## In Sync with the Sacred, Out of Step with the World

Embracing an Unconventional Life
in a Culture of Conformity

TOM STELLA

# In Sync with the Sacred, Out of Step with the World

Embracing an Unconventional Life
in a Culture of Conformity

WOOD LAKE

Editor: Mike Schwartzentruber
Proofreader: Dianne Greenslade
Designer: Robert MacDonald

Cover photograph: Luke Wass

Library and Archives Canada Cataloguing in Publication
Title: In sync with the sacred, out of step with the world :
embracing an unconventional life in a culture of conformity / Tom Stella.
Names: Stella, Tom, author.
Description: Includes bibliographical references.
Identifiers: Canadiana (print) 20200304747 | Canadiana (ebook) 20200305441 |
ISBN 9781773434070 (softcover) | ISBN 9781773431567 (HTML)
Subjects: LCSH: Spirituality. | LCSH: Authenticity (Philosophy) |
LCSH: Self-actualization (Psychology)
Classification: LCC BL624 .S74 2020 | DDC 204/.4—dc23

Unless otherwise noted, all quotations from the Bible are from the New Revised Standard
Version of the Bible, copyright 1989 by the Division of Christian Education of the National
Council of Churches of Christ in the USA. All rights reserved. Used by permission. Bible
quotations marked BSB are from The Holy Bible, Berean Study Bible, BSB Copyright ©2016,
2018 by Bible Hub. Used by Permission. All Rights Reserved Worldwide.

ISBN 978-1-77343-407-0

Published by Wood Lake Publishing Inc.
485 Beaver Lake Road, Kelowna, BC, Canada, V4V 1S5
www.woodlake.com | 250.766.2778

Wood Lake Publishing acknowledges the financial support of the Government of Canada.
Wood Lake Publishing acknowledges the financial support of the Province of British Columbia
through the Book Publishing Tax Credit.

Wood Lake Publishing acknowledges that we operate in the unceded territory
of the Syilx/Okanagan People, and we work to support reconciliation and challenge the
legacies of colonialism. The Syilx/Okanagan territory is a diverse and beautiful
landscape of deserts and lakes, alpine forests and endangered grasslands.
We honour the ancestral stewardship of the Sylix/Okanagan People.

Printed in Canada
Printing 10 9 8 7 6 5 4 3 2 1

# CONTENTS

# DEDICATION

*To my lifelong friend, Ray DeFabio, in whose home
this book was born,
and with whose generous, skillful, and patient
assistance it has come to maturity.*

# EPIGRAPHS

*Generation after generation of men have so lost the sense of an interior life, have so isolated themselves from their own spiritual depths by an exteriorization that has at last ended in complete superficiality, that now we are scarcely capable of enjoying any interior peace and quiet and stability.*

— THOMAS MERTON

*A journey ... goes against the prevailing current. It requires you to step out of line, to break with polite society. Other people will feel the ripples, and they won't like it. Any authentic movement usually requires a break with the past — not because the past is bad, but because it is so difficult for a deeper truth to make itself known among the accretions of habit and conformity.*

— ROGER HOUSDEN

*We live in a culture that begs us to conform. Through its various messages, it calls us to squeeze into its mold. It exerts external pressure on our minds to believe in and buy its opinions, hopes, and aspirations. Yet, the pursuits that define most of our culture never fully satisfy our heart and soul.*

— JOSHUA BECKER

*In every society certain things are regarded as "self-evident truths." Different societies make different assumptions ... but within each society the great majority of the people conform unwittingly to the prevailing set of beliefs.*

— SNELL AND GAIL PUTNEY

# INTRODUCTION

*I went to the woods because I wished to live deliberately,
to front only the essential facts of life, and see if I could
not learn what it had to teach, and not, when I came to die,
discover that I had not lived ... I wanted to live deep and
suck out all the marrow of life ...*
— HENRY DAVID THOREAU

THOREAU, IN HIS CLASSIC
WORK *WALDEN*, GIVES AN ACCOUNT OF THE TWO YEARS
HE SPENT in a small cabin on Walden Pond near Concord,
Massachusetts. It was there he turned his back on society
with its creature comforts and distractions in order to learn
from life, to live authentically, to encounter himself.

I find something compelling about Thoreau's decision
to leave the security of life as he knew it. His desire to "suck
out all the marrow of life," to live close to nature, and to experience the texture of his own thoughts and feelings makes
me want to honestly examine how I live. I want to identify
the beliefs that have kidnapped me from living authentically,
and I want to front fully my penchant to fall into routines of
thought and action that devolve into ruts. I do not want to
come to the end of my days without having lived.

Although Thoreau chose to do so, and despite the fact
that separation from familiar surroundings can be helpful, I

don't believe authentic living necessitates a retreat to the woods. Authenticity is, first and foremost, a matter of being attuned and responsive to the sacred within – to an instinct, an intuition, a sixth sense, a deep voiceless voice that can be "heard" even in a crowd. This inner guide may at times call us to live apart from others, but it surely summons us to follow a road less travelled; that is, it calls us to turn away from the conventional wisdom of society, those ways of thinking, believing, and behaving that go unquestioned – busy is good, more is better, success equals wealth...

Authenticity often requires the courage to be different, to stand out, to be considered odd and perhaps even a threat by those who find their identity, comfort, and security in the status quo. It is nothing less than courageous to live in sync with the sacred because in contrast to honouring the dictates of the soul, living in accord with the conventions of one's family, religion, country, or culture allows us to fit in, to gain the approval of the group, or at least to not experience its disapproval. Because living within the confines of convention satisfies important needs for belonging and acceptance, choosing to walk the different and often lonely path of non-conformity requires the conviction that comes with being rooted in the fertile soil of our soul.

What I intend to share with you here are hints for how to step to the cadence of the sacred – that is, how to approach life in ways that make soul-sense even if they may seem like nonsense to the world around us. In this endeavour I draw from the wisdom of mystics East and West, and from poets, philosophers, and theologians of every ilk, all of whom encourage us to live not only out of step with convention, but in sync with the sacred by whatever name.

Even though I will elaborate on them more fully in the chapters that follow, it may be helpful to mention up front a few words and themes that appear often in the pages of this book.

First, when I use the term "ego" I am not referring to that which we say is big in those who are self-absorbed or who overestimate their attractiveness or talents; I'm afraid that egotistical people have given ego a bad name! My use of "ego" refers to a way of understanding ourselves that is limited to the physical, mental, and emotional aspects of our being. Ego is good, for we need to be strong and healthy in those areas of our self if we are to survive and thrive in this world. But if our self-concept is without a spiritual foundation, it is incomplete, and thus we stand on shaky ground. From this place of "incompleteness," we experience the inadequacy and insecurity that lead us to buy into society's definitions of acceptability and success. If we are not in touch with our spiritual depths, these social definitions can falsely feel like firm footing on which to establish a sense of self.

Second, when I use the word "soul" I am not referring to any "thing." Soul is like psyche; it is intangible but real. Although soul can be a dimension of our self where we encounter our shadow – our fears, insecurities, and pettiness, for example – I generally use the term to refer to the quiet, peaceful, sacred depths wherein we experience the likes of meaning, connection, passion, and compassion. We are attuned to soul when we know there is more to life and to our self than ego-consciousness would have us believe, or that gratification of our senses can satisfy. Soul is the dimension of ourselves about which ego is unaware.

Third, I do not use the word "spiritual" in any religious sense; it is not to be mistaken for devotional piety or New Age thought and practices. Nor do I use the word to refer to a realm above and beyond the human. Spirituality is *not* the opposite of sensuality. Spirituality is a life force, a living, sacred energy that enlivens nature and human nature, creation and creatures. Spirituality is an inner vitality, a sacred dynamism, the life of our soul.

Next, the brand of religion that surfaces in these pages from time to time is not the kind that assumes the existence of a distant, demanding God whom we must please or appease. Religion is not to be associated with any denomination, sect, or faith tradition. Religion is not primarily about doctrine, worship, or rules of behaviour. From the Latin *re ligare*, the word "religion" means to rebind. In its most profound sense, religion has to do with healing a disconnect – the often lost sense of communion with creation, with others, with the deepest dimension of ourselves, and perhaps with a Higher/Inner Power.

Speaking of that "Power," a word about the word "God." For many of us, the word God evokes images of an all-powerful, all-knowing, omnipresent, male deity – a sometimes loving, sometimes angry Supreme Being who is somewhere else (heaven). My use of "God" is more in keeping with theologian Paul Tillich's term "ground of being." In this case, the word God refers to a pervasive spiritual force that is a dimension of our own and all creation's DNA. Though not a person, this reality is personal and intimate as well as infinite. Among the synonyms for God that will appear in this work are Sacred, Mystery, Spirit, Presence, and Higher/Inner Power.

I should also probably say a word about spiritual direction, since like the concepts just mentioned, it will be referred to more than a few times. Spiritual direction is a process wherein two people (director and directee) meet periodically to consider the latter's life from the perspective of her/his soul. (Although it should be understood as a given, I need to say that I have changed the names of all the people I mention in this book in relation to my spiritual direction or counselling practices.) Because spirituality is a thread woven throughout the fabric of life, along with concepts considered traditionally spiritual – such as faith, prayer, and God – some of the content of these sessions may be the same as issues commonly dealt with in counselling: relationships, career, family matters, and the like. However, the point of spiritual direction is not to solve problems or help us to adjust to societal norms; rather, it is to learn from life and to grow more deeply attuned to both its meaning and the direction it may be calling one to take. The goal of spiritual direction is to help a person listen with the ear of their heart, and to open her or him to the sacred proddings that come through instinct, intuition, serendipitous events, mystical moments, tragic occurrences, and the other often subtle and sometimes painful ways in which we are led by a wisdom not our own.

Having said this, I need to alert you to the possibility that you may find some redundancy in the chapters that make up this work. Matters of the soul are pervasive and, if you have an eye for them, they poke their heads from behind almost every rock. As I wrote this book, concepts such as slowing down, being present, facing/embracing life, living with passion, not taking ourselves too seriously, feeling a holy discontent, and honouring ourselves, others, and the earth, kept emerging despite my best efforts to contain them. In any case, I hope this will not seem too repetitious but that, instead, it will serve to reinforce the importance of these concepts for living an authentic life.

Much of what I have written in these pages may appear confounding and, perhaps, controversial; if you find this to be true, I will be pleased. I say this because, as I have already mentioned, living in sync with the sacred often requires walking out-of-step with our culture's unquestioned values and attitudes, which tend to define meaning and success by standards such as affluence, appearance, and accomplishment. Although the figures of great wisdom in every religion and culture are united in exhorting us to live by other values, their message has not always been heeded and has, over time, become domesticated. But the truth remains that we are closest to living well when we listen and respond to the passionate imperatives that arise from deep within.

It has taken some time to emerge, but I have come to discover within myself a two-pronged imperative: my calling to affirm the divinity of humanity, and to assert the sacredness of life in the world. This message appears throughout the book. For much of my life I lived with only one foot in the world, and with a somewhat skeptical view of human nature. I considered the world a proving ground, a place where our task was to win the favour of "the gods" by overcoming our depravity so that the longer stretch that is life-after-death would consist of leisurely rounds at the dessert table in heaven, and not being burned to a crisp in hell.

I now know better. Dessert is being served here every day, as are the not-so-tasty veggies. Life is a sweet and sour banquet, and we are the guests of honour here for the feasting. There is food aplenty; opportunities for nourishment abound. It's time to wake up to the music, to the sumptuous repast, to the mystery that is life in our bodies and in the world. It is too easy to sleep through the festivities, and so I hope that if you need one, this book will serve as a wake-up call.

# ONE

# If a Thing Is Worth Doing, It Is Worth Doing Badly

*Dance like nobody's watching.*

— KATHY MATTEA

**I**T WOULD NOT SURPRISE **ME IF YOUR RESPONSE TO THE TITLE OF THIS CHAPTER** was something like "say what?" or "you're kidding, right?" or "are you jerkin' my chain?" I say this because, like me, you probably feel that things should be done well rather than badly. "Well" just seems like the more familiar, logical, or appropriate word to use at the end of that sentence. When I was given chores as a child, the phrase "be sure you do a good job" often accompanied the assignment; if I did something badly, I had to do it over.

And so I learned early on that anything worth doing was worth doing well and that I should make every effort to excel at whatever I did. If I was not good at something, I would work hard to get better. If I got better, I worked hard to become the best. But even if I wasn't the smartest student in the class, the most proficient athlete on the field, or the best son or brother at home, it was okay as long as I was trying hard to do my best. Mistakes happen, failing is inevitable, imperfection is human, but the thought of being content with doing anything *badly* was not on my radar.

## DOING WHAT WE DON'T DO WELL

Over the years, I've discovered that there are some things I will never do well. I will never, for instance, fathom the complexities of the computer, my smart phone, or any technological gadget for that matter. I will never in a million years be able to calculate my income tax return accurately – just ask my tax accountant. And, in the realm of relationships, the outlook is pretty bleak when it comes to my ever becoming comfortable at the important and often delicate art of confrontation. I realize that I must do some of these things and others like them no matter how poor I am at doing them, and that their difficulty probably has more to do with what the Roman sage Seneca observed: "It's not because things are difficult that we dare not venture. It's because we dare not venture that they are difficult."

I admire people who throw themselves into things they don't think they do well. My brother, Mike, embodies this quality. Mike had little singing experience when he first signed up for a voice class offered through an adult learning program. He enjoyed the teacher and the other students, but the prospect of singing in front of them, a requirement of the class, was daunting. Mike survived this ordeal and made some improvements. He then auditioned for the New Jersey Chorale, a community chorus, and was chosen as a member. After several years and still feeling himself less proficient than others, in part because he could not read music, he nonetheless auditioned for the more high profile Pro Arte Chorale, a semi-professional group and, again, was accepted. To this day Mike doesn't feel he belongs in that league, but he has now sung with Pro Arte at Carnegie Hall and has travelled with them to perform in Liverpool, England.

Life would become very limited if we only did what we do well. Whether in the arenas of love or labour, many of us stumble through the day looking like the silent movie's Keystone Cops. We are a comedy of errors more often than not, a laughing matter much of the time. Everyone I know feels insecure about something they do, but this need not be a problem. What is problematic is giving power to insecurity and never challenging ourselves to reach for higher heights, or venturing into new frontiers. I agree with Rabbi Hillel, a contemporary of Jesus who said, "I get up, I walk, I fall down. Meanwhile I keep dancing." And I affirm the wisdom of Hindu sage Sri Aurobindo who said, "By your stumbling, the world is perfected."

Authors stumble through multiple drafts of their books before getting them published. Athletes stumble – sometimes literally – as they hone their skills. Students and teachers, parents and politicians, carpenters and cooks: everyone does badly, at least for a time, the tasks their roles and professions require. Hard work can keep us from stumbling more often, but I'd like to think that both we and our world are better for our efforts even when they amount to a less than a graceful dance.

## THE NEED FOR APPROVAL

If we accept the wisdom of British literary legend G. K. Chesterton, "if a thing is worth doing it is worth doing badly,"[1] we may feel freer to attempt doing what we don't do well, and we might accomplish things that would otherwise be left undone.

There is a whimsical story about four people: Everybody, Somebody, Anybody, and Nobody. There was an important job to be done and Everybody was sure that Somebody would do it. Anybody could have done it, but Nobody did it. Somebody got angry about that because it was Everybody's job. Everybody thought Anybody could do it, but Nobody realized that Everybody wouldn't do it. It ended up that Everybody blamed Somebody when Nobody did what Anybody could have!

I don't know whether Everybody didn't do what Anybody could have done because he didn't think he could do the job well, but I *do* know that I am more likely to put things off, or avoid doing them altogether, if I'm not good at doing them. This probably has less to do with the task than it does with the fact that I seek approval from others through what I do; given a choice of tasks, I will always choose to do what I think I do well so that I will be well thought of. If the results of my efforts are likely to be mediocre, there is not much of an approval payoff in my doing them.

When approval is a factor in my motivation, when I do something in order to impress others rather than to express what I value, then I will be like Everybody who does not do what Anybody could. But when the worth of what I do is intrinsic to the task and independent of my need for affirmation, whether I do it well or badly is of less consequence, and I am more likely to do what needs to be done.

## THE TYRANNY OF IDEALS

Most of us have some wiggle room when it comes to doing less than our best, but I have discovered that few of us are any good at cutting ourselves slack when we make mistakes or underperform. The problem, I think, is that we succumb to the tyranny of ideals. Ideals are our mind's assessment about what constitutes perfection. Ideals are influenced by the culture – by society, family, religion, and the like – and they are usually a far cry from what is real. Ideals are like stars; we may never reach them, but like a good sailor, we can use them to chart our course.

Ideals are good when we hold them lightly, as they point us in a positive direction and can motivate us to do and to become our best. But if they hold sway over us, ideals have the power to either discourage us from attempting what is difficult, or to put us in a state of chronic discontent when we try but fail to attain them. Carol, one of the people whom I serve as a spiritual director, is a wonderfully kind and generous person. She goes out of her way to anticipate needs, and above and beyond the call in responding to them. Given this, I was surprised when during one of our meetings Carol claimed that she was not a very good person or, from the perspective of her faith tradition, a very good Christian. When I asked her to explain, she referred to times when she wasn't present to friends in need, and also to times when she was present but resented them for wanting her help. In other words, she was unable to recognize her own goodness because she had not achieved her ideal of always being a cheerful giver, one who happily responds to others and never attends to herself unless or until everyone else's needs are met. Sound familiar?

It's easy to see the danger in trying to achieve the ideal of being a cheerful giver, since to live in this manner for long is to court physical, mental, and emotional exhaustion. However, because ideals are often firmly implanted not only in our minds, but in our marrow (we don't learn them, we inhale them), they can dictate the way we think, feel, and act even when we know it's better not to strive for them. Ideals may not only discourage us from doing what we do not do well but, as with Carol, they can also prevent us from seeing how well we do what we do.

## THE DRIVE TO BE PERFECT

Idealism has a roommate whose name is perfection. Many of us are driven by perfectionism, which not only discourages us from doing what we don't do well, but also fuels a sense of inadequacy. Unless it is tempered, perfectionism has the potential to drive us crazy with its demand that we do what we do flawlessly. For the sake of our physical, emotional, and spiritual health, I believe it is imperative that we learn to be content with ourselves as less than perfect.

Monk and mystic Thomas Merton once opined that satisfaction requires contentment with imperfection; this is true not only with regard to our performance, but to our person as well; it applies not just to *what* we do, but to *who* we are.

It may sound strange, but the word *sincere* speaks to this truth. Made up of the two Latin words, *sine cere*, *sincere* literally means "without wax." There may be some question as to the accuracy of its derivation but, as I learned it, the word came about in relation to sculptors and merchants in ancient times. The statues that sculptors sold to merchants often had cracks or small holes. Before selling them to the public, the merchants would melt wax and fill in the flaws. Because the statues then looked perfect, they could be sold at a higher price. To be sincere, then, does not mean "I really mean it," but "I really *am* it." I really am who I really am. I am not *ideal*, but *real*. I am not flawless but filled with imperfections. And I am, despite this fact, good enough.

If our worth resides in our less-than-perfect being rather than in our unblemished appearance or accomplishments, then we are worthwhile even with our physical defects, our mental hang-ups, and our psychological quirks. We are of worth no matter what skin colour or other demographic we identify with: male or female, young or old, rich or poor, gay or straight, believer or atheist. Our attitudes and actions may stand in need of adjustment, but everyone is a worthy being – period.

## CRITICISM IS INHIBITING

It's not only the need for approval, the tyranny of ideals, and the drive to be perfect that can prevent us from undertaking the challenge of doing what we do badly; criticism can produce the same inhibitions.

Liz is a very bright and talented woman whose childhood dreams were never affirmed. When she announced at an early age that she wanted to be president of the United States, her mother promptly told her it would never happen because she was a girl. Later, Liz gave voice to her hope that she would become Miss America, but when a fall resulted in a cut on her knee that required stitches and left a scar, she was told her dream would be impossible. Liz then re-focused her dreams in the direction of becoming a concert pianist, but after making several mistakes at her first recital, and having internalized the critic's voice, she told herself she would never succeed. Despite her many gifts, it is not likely that Liz would have attained any of her dreams even if she had been affirmed, but it is as tragic to be discouraged from dreaming as it is self-defeating to strive after unattainable ideals.

If you are as prone to self-criticism as I am, you may find it easy to leap from the assessment that if you do something badly, you yourself are bad. The fear or experience of failure can easily lead us to feel that we are failures. When so much of our self-worth is measured by what we accomplish, if we fail to produce or perform well, then self-doubt is almost inevitable. But if it is true that anything worth doing is worth doing badly, is it not also true that we are worthwhile even if what we do feels worthless?

I experience the gravitational pull of self-doubt whenever I read evaluations following workshop presentations. Many of my talks are about spirituality in the workplace, a concept that is gaining credibility in the corporate world but that is still far short of being universally valued. There are always people present at my talks who consider the topic, and by association the presenter, irrelevant. Despite the fact that negative feedback is not usually predominant – most people would rather say or write nothing than be critical – I always feel deflated when I read responses that are not affirming, and I always question whether I am a failure and a fraud.

The tendency to be self-critical is not an uncommon response to doing what we do badly, but Chesterton reminds us, even in his dated language, why it is important not to travel far down that road, and to think well of ourselves instead: "All men matter. You matter, I matter. It's the hardest thing in theology to believe."[2] Why is a statement about self worth a matter of theology? Shouldn't Chesterton have said *psychology* instead of *theology*? And, in any case, aren't the natural and supernatural two different realms? Although traditional religious teachings posit a clear separation between divinity and humanity, from a spiritual/mystical perspective the distinction is a blessed blur. Through this lens we see that our significance is not to be found in the flawlessness of what we do, but in the truth that our origin lies in "beginningless" beginnings, and our destiny in eternal endlessness. We matter because we are made in the image and likeness of God, and *God* is a word for the inherent holiness of creation.

## IN SYNC AND OUT OF STEP

"If a thing is worth doing, it is worth doing badly" is surely the prompting of the sacred, as well as a message that is contradictory to our "do-a-good-job" culture. It is not a statement in support of doing a sloppy job, but permission to venture into what we find difficult, to abide our stumbling efforts, and to do our best even at those things we don't do well. When we live in sync with the sacred, we are less prone to the limiting effects of idealism, perfectionism, criticism, and the need for approval. When we are in sync with the sacred, we know we matter, and we are freer to be our *sincere* self. Nobody sets out to do badly what they do, but if what we do is enjoyable, meaningful, or helpful, we would do well to embrace the wisdom of Nike's tagline: "Just do it!"

# TWO

# Life Is Not a One-Piece Puzzle

*Let us train ourselves to desire what
the situation demands.*

— SENECA

LINDA IS A WOMAN IN HER LATE 50S WHO, AFTER RAISING HER FAMILY, began a full-time job and a course of studies leading to a master's degree. Linda loved school; the reading, classroom discussions, and papers she was required to write all gave her life. At one point in a conversation I had with her, she said, "I wish I didn't have to do anything except go to school. I wish all the other responsibilities I have would just go away."

Like many of us, Linda wanted her life to be a one-piece puzzle. Everyone I know, myself included, wants their life to consist only of the things they enjoy most, or the people they want to be around, or the tasks they find meaningful to accomplish. What could be more normal or even healthy than to want our lives to be filled with what makes life a delight?

One of the things that gave me delight as a child was spending time quietly, by myself, playing with a puzzle. I remember searching for the right shapes, sizes, and colours, trying to fit the various pieces into their proper place. Despite or because of their differences, each individual piece contributed to the harmony of the whole. Putting a puzzle together was a matter of trial and error, and although it was sometimes an exercise in frustration, I always experienced a sense of satisfaction when I completed one.

A snapshot of this memory flashed through my mind as Linda spoke. It occurred to me that my own life was less satisfying and less gratifying than it could be because I wanted it to be a one-piece puzzle. I resented the pieces of my life that I did not like. My attempts to control and manipulate my days so that they consisted only of what pleased me most had led to frustration, so I suggested to Linda what I needed to accept myself; namely, that she consider the possibility that every aspect of her life was necessary. Every person, every task, every problem, every interruption, every loss, everything she wished she could wish away was part of what *could* be a harmonious whole, a life filled with a sense of joy, accomplishment, meaning, and satisfaction.

## BURDEN OR BLESSING

I am not an irresponsible person. I am not someone who refuses to perform the tasks that arise from my roles at work, within my family, and in the broader community. But there is a significant difference between *performing* responsibilities and *embracing* them. When I fail to accept and willingly enter into all aspects of my life and, instead, approach them with a reluctant or negative attitude, I end up tired and resentful; my life feels like a chore, a burden rather than a blessing.

The choice between burden and blessing lies before me at this very moment. Writing is a piece of the puzzle of my life that I feel compelled to do but that I wish I could wish away. It is difficult for me to organize my thoughts and to find the words that give expression to them. I dislike this process and am adept at finding creative ways to avoid it. But it is also true that when I accept writing as something I am called to do, and when I focus on its rightness instead of on its difficulty, it becomes a source of satisfaction, and I am left feeling like I did as a child happily lost in putting together a puzzle.

We always have before us the choice between burden and blessing. Each day of our life is filled with things and people we like and dislike, enjoy and resent, find delight in and are drained by. How we choose to deal with our spouse or children, our boss or co-workers, our homework assignments, domestic chores, and so on, can make them a burden or a blessing. Even life's harshest realities – failure, illness, and loss, for instance – can, when fully embraced, become the means through which we experience a strength we didn't know we had, a consoling inner calm, the peace that surpasses understanding. The opposite, of course, is also always true: whatever their shape, size, and colour, when we resist the pieces of our life's puzzle, our days become burdensome.

Better than resisting what we dislike would be to integrate the wisdom of Seneca, who said, "Let us train ourselves to desire what the situation demands." This approach to life is not a denial of the fact that we would rather not deal with some people or situations, but a decision to take life by the horns, to choose a positive attitude toward who and what we encounter, and to not allow ourselves to become mere bystanders watching as our life passes before us unengaged.

## SWEET FOR A MONTH

The difficult pieces of life's puzzle do not always present themselves as such. It is often the case that what looks easy is actually demanding, that what begins sweet eventually turns sour. We speak of the "honeymoon" phase of a new relationship or job, meaning that we have found the ideal person or work situation. But the word *honeymoon* literally means sweet for a month! No thing or person is wonderful forever. Every person and every situation is flawed. But when we are in the honeymoon phase of anything, we want to stay forever in the glow of what feels good. This tendency puts us in good company, for in the gospel story of the Transfiguration (Matthew 17:1–8), it was Peter who, upon seeing Jesus, Moses, and Elijah, longed to stay forever on the mountaintop; he, too, wanted life to be a one-piece puzzle.

When we have lived long enough to experience life's ups and downs, we know the importance of having the honeymoon come to an end. Sweet as they are, honeymoons can prevent us from experiencing what they are a hint of – the bliss that life is meant to be. The paradox, of course, is that bliss is not uninterrupted joy. Rather, it is about becoming people who are capable of being joyful even when life is not.

In our less-than-perfect world, we come to this wisdom only when we have to deal with difficulties. A story is told about a woman who approached a spiritual master hoping he would take away the heartache she felt as a result of her son's death. The master told her she would be cured of her pain if she brought him a mustard seed from the home of someone who did not know suffering. Immediately the woman set out for the village nearby and knocked on the door of the first home she saw. The family welcomed her and soon shared their experience of having to cope with their daughter's mental illness. The woman was moved with pity and, after sharing a meal with them, she left and was granted entry into a house across the road. Before long, that family began to speak of their sadness resulting from the death of a parent. Again, the woman was sympathetic, and again she moved on in the hope of finding a home where there was no suffering. Finally, after encountering similar stories in each of the many homes she visited, she returned to the master without a mustard seed, but with a heart overflowing with compassion.

When the honeymoon is over, when we wake up to the truth that life is sweet for a month – if we're lucky – and when like the woman in this story we have an empty hand but a full heart, we can begin to embrace the once enjoyable, now difficult pieces of our puzzle-like life and become better able to recognize their importance.

## NO PAIN, NO GAIN

Why is there wisdom in the willingness to value all the pieces of our life's puzzle? What is the payoff that comes with opening ourselves to all that is required of us? In the world of strength training there is a saying that is applicable to all of life: "No pain, no gain." If we value growth of body, mind, or spirit, we have to engage in activities that push us to our limits. To become stronger, everything from muscles, to memory, to mettle, must be challenged beyond their current capacity.

If we only and always stay within our comfort zone, we will never develop the full extent of our capabilities. Being an introvert, I am more comfortable alone or dealing one-to-one with people than I am in group settings. Being a "people person," I am more at home in the arena of relationships than I am with technology. Being someone who works with words, I much prefer dialogue to the world of numbers. I could try to arrange it so that I function only in ways that come easily to me, but I fear I would not grow if I were to do so.

As much as I value growth and believe that it usually occurs when I am called beyond comfort, I would rather live by the shortened version of the above saying: "No pain," period! Like I said, I'm not an irresponsible person, but I can be an avoider and a procrastinator. I can, for a while at least, deny the fact that something I'd rather not do needs to be done. When the going gets tough, I sometimes get going – *the other way*. Yet because I have experienced the stagnancy that results when I refuse to be open to that which invites me beyond comfort and complacency, I do not consider it a viable option.

## UNWELCOME FEELINGS

The wisdom of embracing all aspects of our lives applies not only to interpersonal relationships and external situations, it also includes our emotional life. I would like to always be in a good mood. I would like to be positive, enthusiastic, and to see the proverbial glass half full. I would like my emotional life to be a one-piece puzzle; I want to be only and always upbeat. But my reality is otherwise. Like most people, I am prone to down swings and negativity, and I sometimes see flaws and danger where others observe beauty and possibility.

Although I much prefer positive emotions, I have now come to recognize the importance of dark moods and that it's okay, perhaps even necessary, for these unwelcome visitors to take up residence within myself. In his poem "The Guest House," Muslim mystic Jelaluddin Rumi affirms the importance of being open to disturbing thoughts and feelings.

> *This being human is a guest house.*
> *Every morning a new arrival.*
>
> *A joy, a depression, a meanness,*
> *some momentary awareness comes*
> *as an unexpected visitor.*
>
> *Welcome and entertain them all!*
> *Even if they're a crowd of sorrows,*
> *who violently sweep your house*
> *empty of its furniture,*
> *still, treat each guest honorably.*
> *He may be clearing you out*
> *for some new delight.*
>
> *The dark thought, the shame, the malice,*
> *meet them at the door laughing,*
> *and invite them in.*
>
> *Be grateful for whoever comes,*
> *because each has been sent*
> *as a guide from beyond.*[1]

When we resist the temptation to make our life, both within and without, a one-piece puzzle, we become students of life. Everything, everyone, and every aspect of our being can teach us lessons of humility and compassion, of patience and openness. If Rumi is right, even the fluctuations of our inner life, our emotional ups and downs, "a joy, a depression, a meanness," can teach us that we must go with the flow of our heart's vacillations if we are to experience "some new delight."

It has been said that a happy person is someone who can enjoy the scenery on a detour! If we accept the fact that all the pieces of our life's puzzle are necessary in order to make us whole and complete, we can experience the "new delight" of beauty, surprise, and insight even when we are re-routed, even when the road we want to travel is closed, even when life both inside and out becomes puzzling. Failure as well as success, pain as well as pleasure, the difficult as well as the effortless, have a place in creating the harmonious whole that our life can be.

## HOME AT LAST

Thus far I have used the image of a one-piece puzzle as a metaphor to indicate our preference for those aspects of life, both external and internal, we find most pleasing. Using the same metaphor, we can also come to understand our whole self as one piece of a larger, sacred puzzle.

Poet Robert Frost said, "Home is the place where, when you have to go there, they have to let you in."[2] When our time on earth is complete, I'd like to think that we find our place, our home as it were, in the puzzle, the mystery, sometimes named God. What if Mystery in this sense, what if the word God, refers not only to an omnipresent spiritual reality here and now, but also to the puzzling Presence in which and to which we belong when we no longer belong here – a reality that has to let us in? What if we're just the right shape, size, and colour to help complete the Mystery that awaits our homecoming? Perhaps the discontent we experience here, the longings that nothing and no one can satisfy, the inner-emptiness that cannot be filled, will find fulfillment as the piece of the puzzle that we are settles into its divine resting place – home at last, free at last. This is all conjecture, of course, but as the Beach Boys sing, "Wouldn't it be nice?"

## IN SYNC AND OUT OF STEP

To want our life to be a one-piece puzzle is as natural as breathing. Whether we know it or not, we are inclined to arrange our lives so that everything we do, everyone we are with, and every emotion we experience falls within our comfort zone. "No pain" is both our own and our culture's refrain; we want the "honeymoon" phase of life to last forever. But the sacred invites us to embrace all that comes our way and, at times, to seek that which stretches us beyond our limits. When we are in sync with the sacred, we have the power to transform every burden into a blessing, and, if we heed its call, our lives might become both a harmonious whole here and a taste of our home in the hereafter.

# THREE

# Don't Just Do Something, Stand There

*Be where you is, 'cuz if you ain't where you is,*
*you is where you ain't.*

— JAMES FINLEY

THE F. D. STELLA PRODUCTS
CO. WAS A FOOD EQUIPMENT DEALERSHIP IN DETROIT,
MICHIGAN, FOR OVER 60 YEARS. During high school I, along
with some of my siblings and cousins, spent the summers
working for the family business. One of our assignments was
to work on the dock loading and unloading shipments. My
father was in charge of that part of the operation. When he
would catch us taking a breather, he would sometimes say,
"If you had three hands, your mothers would have to sew
another pocket on your pants!" It's true – we weren't the hardest workers in the company, but it's also true that *any* amount
of hands-in-pockets standing around and shooting the breeze
was unacceptable. Hard and constant work was the order of

the day. If my father had ever heard the Zen saying, "Don't just do something, stand there," he would've been astounded. In his mind, "standing there" was equivalent to loitering, which constituted grounds for arrest, even if – or especially if – you were family!

Because our culture values work over leisure and self-reflective time, standing still is less acceptable than doing just about anything. Busyness is a virtue and when someone claims to be "crazy busy" the statement is more often a form of bragging than a complaint. If someone is crazy busy, they must be *really* important!

## IT CAN BE HARD TO STAND THERE

It not only goes against the grain of our culture to think of standing or sitting still as valuable, but for some people it's nearly impossible. In my spiritual direction practice, I have a number of directees who are clearly Type A personalities – tightly wound individuals who are hard-wired to be constantly on the go. Although they value the life of their soul and the spiritual direction process that can help them become attuned to it, Type A folks have a hard time slowing down enough to sense their spiritual depth and the sacredness of life – realities that are easily overlooked when we are moving through the day at warp speed. Sometimes I think it may be more difficult for a Type A person to meditate than it would be to drive a Buick through a keyhole!

Meditation is a proven way of slowing down that involves what can feel like long periods (20 minutes give or take) of sitting still. Meditation is a way to still not only our body, but our mind as well. There are various methods of meditation, but paying attention to each breath or the silent recitation of a repetitive word or phrase (a mantra), are among the most common means used to slow down and become still. Don, one of my Type A directees, reported his difficulty with meditation. He talked about being fidgety and about how his "monkey mind" would race a mile-a-minute, swinging from one unrelated thought to another. I think Don expected me to criticize him, or to encourage him to try harder, but instead I simply suggested he stop trying to meditate.

Even though meditation is a way of "standing there" and, as such, is an important spiritual practice for many people, for Don it had become a chore, just a different form of "doing something." For some people, trying to be still really does seem to be more work than working, and so I suggest that they look for another way to be still, one that honours their temperament. This is often referred to as mindfulness.

## LIVING MINDFULLY

Mindful living is a way of "standing there," or of practicing "stillness," even as we are doing something. Mindfulness is about being fully present to the moment, to the people we are with and to the tasks at hand. When we live mindfully, we become more aware of what we usually do automatically, more appreciative of what we take for granted, and more conscious of the sacredness of simple things. A story is told about a spiritual teacher who, when asked by one of his students about Buddhism, replied, "We stand, we sit, we bathe, and we walk."

The questioner responded, "I do those things too."

The master replied, "When we stand, we *know* we are standing ..."

Living with this depth of awareness can turn our everyday actions into spiritual practices, for *knowing* is more than knowledge; it is sensual sensitivity to the sacred hidden in plain sight. Though they are often considered opposites, sensuality and spirituality are sides of the same sacred coin.

The kind of knowing referred to in the above story is a whole-person consciousness, an awareness that involves all our senses. I think it is rare that we are fully conscious of all that our senses take in, and I suspect that what was said in one of the biblical psalms about the statues people misguidedly worshipped may apply to us: "They have eyes, but cannot see. They have ears, but cannot hear" (Psalm 135:16–17, BSB).

Using the sense of sight to demonstrate this point, isn't it amazing how easily we can look at something but not see it? I live in Colorado Springs, in the shadow of Pike's Peak. I look at that mountain from my living room window every day, but I can go months without really seeing it; that is, without being moved by the wonder of its being. If this is true of a 14,000-foot mountain, it can certainly be true of things that are much less imposing – including people. Familiarity may not breed contempt as the adage claims, but it can easily result in blindness to the sacredness of those with whom we live and work.

For most readers, the following exercise will demonstrate how easily we fail to see what is before us.

*Read the statement below.*
> FINISHED FILES ARE THE RESULT
> OF YEARS OF SCIENTIFIC STUDY
> COMBINED WITH THE EXPERIENCE
> OF MANY YEARS.

*Now read it again taking note of how many times you see the letter F.*

*(When I use this exercise in workshops and retreats, most people see only three F's. When I ask them to read it again, most still see*

*only three, or whatever number they first observed. But there are*
*actually six F's.)*
*If you did not see six F's, you did not see them all. Look again.*
*If you continue to see fewer than six, look for the word "OF,"*
*which appears twice in the second line and once in the last line!*

"Standing there" is about being wherever we are. It need not require physical stillness, but it *does* necessitate full awareness of the present moment lest we overlook the often subtle but pervasive spiritual Presence that permeates all things – the f in the word *of*. But even if we should fail to see or sense it, that Presence is present – we live always on the surface of boundless Mystery.

## SLOW DOWN, YOU'RE MOVIN' TOO FAST

Zen teacher Jon Kabat-Zinn is the author of the book *Wherever You Go, There You Are*. That statement may appear obvious, but its simplicity is deceiving. We may be somewhere bodily, but because we are more than physical beings (we are essentially spiritual), we may not be fully *present* spiritually or even emotionally just because we happen to be where we are physically. Full presence requires not only an awareness of where we are, of what we are doing, who we are with, and what is taking place around us, but also a sensitivity and vulnerability to the spiritual essence of all that is, in all its miraculous simplicity.

When speaking about being present, my friend and spiritual teacher Jim Finley says whimsically, "Be where you is, 'cuz if you ain't where you is, you is where you ain't!" It can be dangerous when we ain't where we is, because accidents are more likely to happen. Have you ever "come to" while driving your car? If you've ever had that experience, you know exactly what I'm talking about. But when we are where we is, we are not only safer, we are more likely to experience the spiritual richness of reality. This is expressed well by priest-psychologist Anthony de Mello who says, "If you look at a tree and see a tree, you have really not seen the tree. When you look at the tree and see a miracle – then, at last, you have seen!"[1]

Many of us have become good at doing several things at the same time (multi-tasking), and at high speeds. We live not only by the adages "the sooner the better" and "the more the better," but also "the faster the better." There is nothing wrong with speed *per se*, or with being adept at doing many things at once, but living in this manner contradicts mindfulness, can cause us to miss life's many minor miracles, and takes a toll on our bodies; we become worn-out physically, stressed-out mentally, and burnt-out emotionally. We are people, not machines. When we try to do too much too fast for too long, not only does the quality of our work suffer, every part of us suffers.

## CASUALTIES OF BUSYNESS

Living on the run can adversely affect not only our individual selves, but our relationships. When we don't linger with one another, we tend not to talk about the significant, non-practical dimensions of our lives – matters of the heart. I have limited experience in South America, but on a fact-finding trip to Chile in the early 1980s, a time when the country was struggling politically and economically, I witnessed the relational benefits of a slow-paced society. The inhabitants of the *publaciones* (shanty towns) where I stayed were remarkably present to each other and to those of us who were visiting. They were not in a hurry to go anywhere or to do anything other than attend to the demands of the moment. In First World countries, we spend a lot of time watching our watches, while in many poorer countries people watch, and watch out for each other.

In some cultures, a slower pace of life is just the way things are. I have a plaque hanging on my kitchen wall that says in Spanish, ¡*Que bonito es no hacer nada y después de no hacer nada descansar*! "What a beautiful thing it is to do nothing, and after doing nothing, to rest!" My father would have been dumbfounded!

In Italy, which compared to most cultures is pretty laid-back, a movement called "slow down" has arisen to address the problems associated with the fast life. Its focus is primarily on food preparation and eating – here we call it the "slow food movement" – but high-speed living has filtered into many aspects of that usually nonchalant culture. Having been to Italy several times, I can attest that meals are generally eaten leisurely, but the pace of traffic in the large cities rivals anything I have seen in this country. "Slow Life" is a similar movement in Japan that advocates slowing down in order to rediscover the interconnectedness of people and our relatedness to the earth. At this writing, "slow down" and "slow food" movements have upwards of 80,000 members in over 100 nations.

"Standing there" and slowing down are difficult concepts to recognize as positive in our culture, in part because we place such a high premium on productivity. If we are not productive, we are not considered worthwhile; we're simply taking up space rather than earning our place on the planet. But there are good reasons to be still, or to go at life more slowly, one of which is that it allows us to tap into creativity, something that is a casualty of a fast-paced life. In his book *Taking Flight*, Anthony de Mello relates the following story.

An efficiency expert was making his report to Henry Ford.

*"As you will see sir, the report is highly favorable except for the man down the hall. Every time I pass by he's sitting with his feet on his desk. He's wasting your money."*

*Said Ford, "That man once had an idea that earned us a fortune. At the time I believe his feet were exactly where they are now."*[2]

Efficiency has an obvious value when it comes to work; getting more done in less time and with the least amount of effort makes great practical sense. But if there is no time to dream about what might someday be, and no time to think about what could be improved upon, not only our individual work but our work culture will be the poorer.

## A QUIET, ORDERED LIFE

Every spiritual tradition places high value on living a quiet, ordered life. This is so because living in this manner makes it more likely that we will be poised to experience the extraordinary nature of ordinary life. Meals may be a good illustration of this point.

My guess is that most of us do not experience eating a meal as something spiritual. We eat in order to nourish our bodies and, when we share a meal with others, eating can become a ritual that serves to nourish our relationships. But if we are starving, if in the chaos of our day we have missed one or more meals, we may not be in a condition to savour the sacredness of the meal, or of the companions – from the Latin *cum panis* "with bread" – with whom we share it. It is when we attend to our physical, mental, and emotional needs in a constant manner that we can enter into meals, relationships, or any other aspect of life not with a need to devour, but as a form of devotion.

Living a quiet and ordered life enables us to sense our oneness with the universal Self that priest-paleontologist Teilhard de Chardin refers to as "being within the within of all creation." This awareness can reveal the divine depths that lie at the heart of our most common, everyday activities – from eating, to working, to walking, to talking.

The apparent "standing there" that is a quiet, ordered life is actually a spiritual activity, a journey of sorts that moves us from the surface to the sacred centre of life. This was the case for the hermit in the following story.

There was a young man who, although he valued the spiritual life, felt that it necessarily involved doing acts of charity. He heard about a hermit not far from where he lived who did nothing but contemplate all day. Frustrated by the thought of such a one-dimensional life, the young man called on the hermit, who invited him to enter his holy space.

"How can you just sit here all day?" the youth demanded.

"I'm not sitting here," the hermit replied, "I'm on a journey."

It is no small paradox, but when it comes to the life of our soul, standing there is doing something and slowing down is the fastest way to get where we are going.

As I write these words, I am in a monastery: Genesee Abbey, near Rochester, New York. The abbey is home to about 35 Trappist monks, several of whom live as hermits apart from the rest of the community. Many people I know feel the life of monks, not to mention hermits, is useless, because they appear to contribute nothing to society. But I have found that those who live a cloistered life are truly on a journey, and that in doing so they witness to the rest of us the importance of attending to our souls. I am convinced that if we were to heed the lesson their lives offer, if we were faithful in our own less secluded way to the spiritual life, doing something *less* often and standing there *more* often would be the beginning, at least, of a great transformation – of our lives, our families, our workplaces, our cities, our countries, and the world.

## IN SYNC AND OUT OF STEP

When we just "stand there"; when we slow down; when we live a quiet, ordered life, we find ourselves in sync with the sacred and out of step with the world. It is not busyness we value in so doing, but life; it is not accomplishments we strive for, but a quality of presence to those who share with us the mystery of existence; it is not a destination we seek, but the experience of a quiet journey that leads to our soul. Even if we are a Type A personality or are burdened with many responsibilities, this mindful approach to life can enable us to sense in the ordinariness of our everyday work and relationships the *f* in *of* – the subtle presence of the Presence for which we long.

# FOUR

# Lighten Up

*Laughter is carbonated holiness.*

— ANNE LAMOTT

I ARRIVED AT THE AIRPORT IN SAN DIEGO ONE WARM, SUNNY DAY – are there any other kinds of days there? – and stepped out of the terminal to catch a shuttle to the rental car lot. In a booth marked "Transportation Information," I noticed a sign that has stayed at the forefront of my mind since that day decades ago: "Everyone brings joy to this office, some when they come and others when they leave."

Everyone brings with them – to their home, workplace, or wherever they go – a presence that is joyful, positive, caring, interested and interesting – or not. People are either happy to be with us, or happy to be without. Think for a moment about the people who bring joy to your office or your life. I'm not just referring to those who have a good sense of humour or a ready joke for every occasion. I'm talking about people who make you feel at home in their presence, who affirm you as someone of value without necessarily saying a word.

We can help people feel special by giving them our undivided attention, by listening deeply, and by making eye contact and the like, but my guess is that many of those who make us feel important have that effect on us because they've taken to heart G. K. Chesterton's statement, "Angels can fly because they take themselves lightly."[1] Experience has taught me that when someone would rather see our backside going out the door than have us remain in their presence, it is often because we take ourselves and life too seriously. Since the world is always something of a mess, and because life constantly presents us with challenges in the form of personal trials and tribulations, it is easy to be afflicted with a case of terminal seriousness.

## COMPASSION FOR OUR SELF

Because joy is a byproduct of taking ourselves lightly, it is an antidote for the dis-ease of terminal seriousness. Frivolous may be the opposite of serious, but joy is its corrective. One definition of joy is that it is compassion turned inward. Like many people, I find it easier to be gentler with others than with myself. I bend over backwards to understand and accept the shortcomings of other people, but one small slip, one instance of forgetting where I put something, one failure to achieve a goal or live up to my own or another's expectation, and I'm all over myself with criticism. Compassion turned inward is an art I've not yet mastered.

Several people come to my mind when I think of those who seem not to share my penchant for self-criticism, and who have brought a sense of joy to my life, but Joe stands out. He was my spiritual director during the year I spent in a masters program in Berkeley, California. Joe is a Jesuit priest, a psychologist, and he also happens to be gay. Because of his progressive views on theology, his relaxed attitude toward religious rules, and his sexual orientation, Joe has been out of sync with the Catholic church, with the ethos of his religious community, with some members of his own family, and with society in general his entire life. In learning to deal with these life challenges, Joe has become a person so at home with himself, so comfortable in his own skin, that it is difficult not to feel at ease in his presence.

Because I was serious about growing spiritually and emotionally, I approached my spiritual direction sessions with Joe in a less-than-frivolous manner. He patiently tolerated the fact that I always brought to him an array of problems that I felt were getting in the way of my progress toward becoming more peaceful and prayerful, and I always left him feeling better than when I came, even though my perceived problems remained. What I began to realize over time was that I was too serious about serious things; I was the problem. But even more helpful than this insight was the realization that my being "the problem" didn't *have* to be a problem. So I'm not perfect. So what? Who cares? Lighten up!

## WHO CARES?

There's a Zen story about a student who, before going on an extended journey in search of enlightenment, promised his teacher that he would send a written account of his progress each month. At the end of the first month he wrote, "I feel an expansion of consciousness and I experience my oneness with the universe."

The teacher crumpled up the paper and threw it away.

At the end of the second month another missive arrived: "I have discovered the divine presence in all things."

The teacher was bitterly disappointed.

Month three brought this statement: "The mystery of the one and the many has been revealed to my wondering gaze."

The teacher fell asleep while reading this note.

At the end of the next month the student wrote, "No one is born, no one lives, no one dies, for the self is not."

The teacher threw up his hands in despair.

Month five brought no message from the student, so the teacher wrote to remind him of his promise.

In response the student wrote, "Who cares?"

The teacher stood up, hands lifted to the sky and exclaimed, "At last he's got it!"

Like the student in this story, and like me when I met with Joe, many of the people I see in spiritual direction are too serious about becoming more spiritual, more prayerful, more holy. It is no small paradox that although nothing is more important to the life of our soul than becoming more spiritually attuned, a "Who cares?" attitude is the best way to achieve that end.

The desire to become more spiritual reveals our ignorance of the fact that we are already deeply spiritual beings. Spiritual growth is less a matter of becoming someone we have yet to become and more about realizing who we are already. It is not primarily about having lofty insights or extraordinary experiences, but is more often a subtle waking up to the spiritual nature of ourselves, others, and all things ordinary. This awakening is not something we achieve by our efforts. Rather, it is a matter of yielding to the holy hunch that divinity is the D in our DNA. It is also the sobering realization of how rarely we are in touch with this seminal truth.

Being too serious about becoming spiritual can be a problem, but is it possible to be too serious about becoming lighthearted? I believe the answer to this question is "yes," because lightheartedness is not so much a goal to attain as it is a way of being while we're on the way to whatever goals we have. This is reminiscent of an adage associated with the peace movement: "There is no way to peace, peace is the way." If we hold lightly – not tightly – the things we value and for which we strive, we are already home, already emanating the lighthearted joy that makes others happy to have us around, and that makes it easier for us to be around ourselves.

## CUT YOURSELF SOME SLACK

It has been said that the road to enlightenment is long and difficult, so don't forget snacks and a magazine! As we journey along the road of life, moving by fits and starts toward becoming who and how we want to be, we have to cut ourselves some slack lest we become discouraged at our slow progress.

I am embarrassed when I realize how hard it is for me to practice what I preach in this regard. One of the things I enjoy most is travelling to different cities to give talks or lead retreats and workshops. More specifically, what I like is the opportunity to have the privacy and quiet seclusion of the places where I stay. I always look forward to this solitary time as a mini-retreat, and as a time to accomplish work that is difficult to do in the midst of familiar surroundings and day-to-day demands. But what happens more often than not is that when I get to my room at the end of the day, I pick up the television remote and channel surf until I fall asleep! The next morning my initial instinct is to give my-self a hard time for not following through with my more productive plans, but deeper down I know that along with snacks and a magazine, a few television shows have their place on the journey.

There are worse things than being serious about spiritual growth, but unless we learn to lighten up we may miss out on much that life has to offer and, in our self-preoccupation, we may overlook opportunities to respond to the needs of others. Our awareness of and response to the people we encounter is what matters most, for it has always been the case that love of neighbour trumps the likes of striving for purity, piety, and perfection.

## LAUGHTER IS CARBONATED HOLINESS

Laughter and lightheartedness are not synonymous, but they often exist in proximity to one another; laughter releases endorphins which have long been known to have a beneficial effect on our bodies as well as on our minds and hearts. A well-documented example of this can be found in author Norman Cousin's book *Anatomy of an Illness*, where he relates how he laughed himself to recovery from a terminal illness by watching videos of his favourite comedians.

Laughter not only aids our own healing, it can also help create harmony in our relationships. Musician and humorist Victor Borge said that laughter is the shortest distance between two people. This is true no matter how different or difficult people or peoples may be. Laughter and lightheartedness are the same in every language and can bridge gaps, create common ground, and diffuse tension. I can't help but think the world would be a better place if politicians and world leaders would laugh more – at themselves, and with each other.

Nothing makes lightening up more difficult or more important than tension. Tension wreaks havoc on our bodies, minds, and hearts faster than anything I know, and it can also ruin the happiest occasions. Some years ago, I was asked to preside at the wedding of a former student in Chicago. As is often the case, one set of parents was divorced and so there was some tension in the prospect of both parents attending the marriage of their son. That stress was heightened when the groom's father failed to arrive on time for the rehearsal. As we were concluding, he hurried through the door of the church breathless and said apologetically, "When I got off the plane, I hailed a cab and told the driver to take me to St. Michael's, but instead of bringing me here to the church, he took me to Michael Jordan's restaurant!" A true story that diffused the tension and set a positive tone for the rest of the weekend.

Author Anne Lamott says laughter is carbonated holiness! I believe we are at our spiritual best when we laugh. When we laugh we are not self-conscious, but spontaneous; we do not worry what effect our laughter will have on others, we are worry-free. There is no such thing as serious laughter, unless we are talking about the doubled over, fall-off-your-chair experience that happens all too rarely – often at times and places where we should be more restrained! Like joy, laughter is a byproduct of lightness; and lightness, even in the face of the sober realities of life, is a sign of spiritual health.

## LIGHTNESS IN THE FACE OF DEATH

It may be hard to imagine, but we can be lighthearted even in the face of death. British playwright George Bernard Shaw reminds us of this truth when he says, "Life does not cease to be funny when people die anymore than it ceases to be serious when people laugh."[2] To be lighthearted does not mean we deny the serious nature of life or death, for both are dimensions of the amazing mystery of being. Life is sacred and it is fitting to experience it with a heart open to both its joys and sorrows. Death, our own and others', is likewise sacred, and despite whatever sadness we might feel in its presence, it may also be embraced with a sense of hope. No matter what occasions it, death might be nothing less than the experience of the disappearance of life's limits, a free fall into the bliss of endless being.

I don't think I have ever feared death, but I have always had a fear of life because of death. When I was young, my parents told stories about how they were orphaned at an early age. In fact, the stories are some of my earliest memories. My paternal grandfather drowned at a picnic following the baptism of his 13th child. My grandmother died nine months later of a broken heart. My maternal grandfather died in the 1918 flu epidemic eight months before my mother was born; she was five years old when her mother died.

I grew up feeling and fearing life's precariousness. I carried into adulthood a need to protect myself from the dangers that lurked omnipresent and that had the power to break both my body and my heart. Although vestiges of that fear remain, I now find it possible to live and to love in the face of it. Living freely and loving fully are indications that the process of lightening-up is taking place.

When we lighten up, we are freed up, liberated to live and to love despite the inevitability of loss. Commenting on this truth and on poet David Whyte's work entitled "Self Portrait," poet and author Roger Housden says,

*The ego, the personal identity that is constructed around our own needs and wants and fears, is always defeated by love ... apart from our daily fears and failures, there will always be death which will scatter our dreams and our loves like dust in a strong wind.*[3]

Although death has the power to break our heart, it need not break our soul. Death separates us physically from the people we love, but as author and columnist Mitch Albom has said, death ends a life, but not a relationship; we remain united in soul even in our separateness. This is what makes it possible to lighten up in the face of death and to affirm that "life does not cease to be funny when people die."

## IN SYNC AND OUT OF STEP

When we walk the earth with a light heart, we are in sync with the sacred. There is much in life that needs to be taken seriously, much that requires concern and effort if both we and our world are to thrive. But gravitas without gratitude for the good can darken any endeavour. It may be courageous to resist the temptation to go at life with a heavy heart and furrowed brow, but self-compassion and a healthy "who cares" attitude can rescue us from being terminally serious. When we live with an enlightened awareness of the sacredness of our own life and of all life, we bring an aura of joy to the places we visit and the people we encounter.

# FIVE

# Pain Is Inevitable, Suffering Is an Option

*Not everything that is faced can be changed,*
*but nothing can be changed until it is faced.*

— JAMES BALDWIN

LIFE IS DIFFICULT" IS THE FIRST SENTENCE OF PSYCHIATRIST M. SCOTT PECK'S BOOK *THE ROAD LESS TRAVELED.* This statement is both undeniably true and universally experienced. Along with being wonderful, exciting, fulfilling, and gratifying, life is also difficult. Life can be challenging and exasperating. More often than not, life tries our patience and tests our faith. Whether we're talking about physical, mental, emotional, or spiritual matters, life can be unfair, maddening, and heartbreaking. This may be more true for some than others, but we all have our share of difficulties, whether these are caused by others, or are self-inflicted, or the result of natural events. Life is difficult, and pain is inevitable.

The generally accepted understanding of *suffering* is that it is pain on steroids. When we say someone suffers from migraines, cancer, Alzheimer's, or depression, we usually mean their pain is intense, prolonged, and possibly chronic. However, when I use the word suffer here, I'm not referring to pain writ large, but to its meaning in the Latin – *sufferre* means to "bear up," or "to endure." Suffering in this sense refers to how we carry our pain. We can resist the reality of our pain and resent its causes and consequences, or we can embrace it.

Pain may be inevitable, but we can choose how we deal with it; we can do so grudgingly or gracefully, though I know the latter is a bit of a stretch. As a hospital and hospice chaplain, I have witnessed both kinds of suffering in patients who experience physical pain. Some carry their pain with dignity, not denying or minimizing it, and not allowing it to sour their attitude or the manner in which they relate to medical staff, or to their family and friends. Others, some of whom are actually in less acute pain, both resist and resent their condition thus becoming *a pain* to themselves and to others.

As a priest, counsellor, and spiritual director, I have also observed the different ways people deal with non-somatic pain. The distress of loss and loneliness is no picnic. A heartache is every bit as real as a headache. The spiritual pain known as the "dark night of the soul" is a dis-ease as palpable as any other.

In all these situations, it can be a good thing to express one's anger and frustration at no longer feeling whole and healthy, but some turn this phase of the grieving process into a lifestyle. People can become identified with their pain;

they become their anger and, as a result, they end up being bitter. Others, those who carry their pain well, allow it to teach them about life and about their need to rely on other people, and maybe also on a Higher/Inner Power.

## ATTITUDE AND FAITH

Why do some people suffer their pain in creative, life-giving ways while others do not? In his classic book *Man's Search for Meaning*, holocaust survivor and psychoanalyst Victor Frankl claims that despite the inability to change his circumstance, the freedom to choose his attitude toward it enabled him and others to endure the horrors of the concentration camps. Frankl wrote, "everything can be taken from a man but one thing: the last of the human freedoms – to choose one's attitude in any given set of circumstances ..."[1] When we choose to embrace our pain and refuse to be a victim of it, we are more likely to find the strength to bear it well.

But this begs a question: What makes it possible to accept our pain rather than rail against it? What gives us the courage to maintain a positive attitude in the face of physical, emotional, or spiritual pain? For a great many people, faith can be a difference maker. For some people, it is the traditional religious belief that those who experience pain and sorrow now will be rewarded in the life to come. Whether this is true or even good theology is debatable, but this belief can give meaning to a life of pain which, in turn, can help make it bearable. Those who hold this conviction often point to the Beatitudes for biblical confirmation: "Blessed are those who mourn, for they shall be comforted" (Matthew 5:4).

But there is another expression of faith that can result in the same ability to suffer well the pain that comes our way. This faith has nothing to do with an afterlife, but everything to do with the rewards of living with integrity here and now. This kind of faith is not about believing in a "just" God, or in some sort of *quid pro quo* exchange of present pain for future bliss. Rather, I am speaking of faith as a conviction that our deepest pain has the potential, the power, to bring new life.

I am aware of no greater pain than that of parents who experience the death of a child. I had just finished presiding at the last of three masses one Sunday morning when my pager went off; the call was from a chaplain at the hospital where I worked. Theresa informed me that a couple whose son was brought to the emergency room was asking for me. When I arrived at the hospital, my friends John and Rita greeted me with the heartbreaking news that their 28-year-old son had died. Over time, as the shock of his tragic and untimely death began to wear off, John and Rita sank into a deep grief that bordered on depression. Years later, when speaking with them about that period of their lives, I asked what made it possible for them to get through it. They told me it was their faith, their conviction that Paul, their son, had lived a full even if too-brief life. They were buoyed by the realization that he loved life and was always true to himself. The vibrant manner with which Paul lived taught them that they must embrace even his death with openness to its being a new dimension of life for him and for them.

## RUN TO THE ROAR

Some people face their pain while others run from it. The former is about accepting everything life has to offer, while the latter makes us victims of life's randomness. Acceptance is not masochism; it does not mean we would rather know pain than pleasure, or sorrow than joy. Facing pain means we are open to experiencing *everything* that being wedded to the world entails, the good times and bad, the easy times and the difficult times.

When we try to deny or refuse to accept what is painful, we live like a boxer, bobbing and weaving in an attempt to avoid the jabs and the inevitable knockout punch life will throw at us. Those who live like this know that pain is inevitable and that death will throw the last punch. They know that life, as one definition has it, is a sexually transmitted terminal condition – you'd just never know it by the way they move around the ring!

Paradoxically, it is more dangerous to try to avoid pain, and the fear of it, than it is to face into it, as the following story illustrates. When a male lion who is the leader of the pride grows too old to hunt, it still has value in the pride's quest for food. The old lion positions himself at one end of the meadow where the prey is grazing, while the rest of the pride hides at the other end. Although he is no longer able to attack, the old lion is still capable of emitting a ferocious sound. When the time is right, he lets out a blood-curdling roar from which the prey instinctively runs away – into the claws and the jaws of the waiting pride.

Novelist and social critic James Baldwin says, "Not everything that is faced can be changed, but nothing can be changed until it is faced."[2] Whether or not painful circumstances can be changed, our best option is to run to the roar, to move toward pain. Try to relax into the bodily ache. Confront the discomfort of a strained relationship. Sit still in the abyss of loneliness. Allow the doubt and the darkness that blankets the soul from time to time to have its day. It is amazing how pain, though still present, becomes more tolerable when we suffer it well.

A friend once told me that, in his experience, although pain that is embraced doesn't go away, "something shifts." He couldn't describe the "something," and he couldn't pinpoint exactly what he meant by the word "shifts," but he was clear that when he stopped resisting the pain it became made it less painful and easier to bear. This is what is meant by the saying, "When you walk into the fire, you find out it's raining in there!"

## SUFFERING THE PAIN OF OTHERS

How we choose to suffer our own pain makes it more or less difficult to bear. But we also have an option when it comes to dealing with the pain of others. We can attempt to cure them, or we can attempt to care for them; that is, we can accompany them in their suffering. Of course, this may not be an either/or matter, as we can be caring at the same time that we administer healing balms, physical or otherwise.

When a cure is not possible, however, when there is no hope for recovery in sight, when everything that can be done has been done to alleviate pain and to facilitate health, there is still another option that can be helpful – this is the way of compassion.

From the Latin *cum pati*, compassion means "to suffer with." When we are truly present to those who are in pain, when we don't try to minimize or spiritualize what they are feeling but instead acknowledge the fear or anger that often arise in the face of hopelessness, helplessness, and distress, our understanding and willingness to share in their pain can be transformative. It has been said that shared joy is increased, and shared pain is lessened. Sharing the pain of others can lighten their load and enable them to suffer it more gracefully, for they then have the consoling and sustaining realization that they are not alone.

It is nothing less than courageous to accompany a person in the midst of pain that cannot be cured. Caregivers who attend to the needs of the seriously or terminally ill often do so at the cost of their own health. They also do so at the cost of their convenience. I witnessed this first-hand as my mother cared for my father in the last years of his life, and as my sister cared for our dying mother. Caring for another is a gruelling experience physically and emotionally, but the rewards are worth the cost, for we usually receive more than we give – a truth that is often realized only in retrospect.

You have likely heard the saying that it is more blessed to give than to receive. This may be true, but I have come to believe that receiving is more difficult; a reality I have witnessed time and time again while visiting patients in the hospital. Sometimes their pain was not primarily the result of their physical condition. Rather, it was because their situation threatened their sense of independence; it did not allow them to care for others and they were put in the humbling position of having to allow others to care for them. This type of pain may not be inevitable, for there are people who tolerate and even enjoy being attended to, but many of us have to swallow our pride and let go of our need to serve in order to suffer this "ill-at-easeness" with dignity. It need not be demeaning to have to receive help, but it is often humbling. It is a difficult lesson, but learning to be a grateful and gracious receiver is a wonderful complement to being a gracious giver.

## IN SYNC AND OUT OF STEP

"Shit happens" is a not-so-delicate way of saying life is difficult. But in the midst of life's travails there is a way to navigate that makes pain bearable; we can choose to suffer it. We respond to the sacred whenever we choose this path; and, whenever we embrace life's difficult times with faith, we discover that they are often the font from which comes new life.

It is a natural and sometimes very necessary instinct to try to avoid or alleviate pain. Many times in life, however, there is great wisdom in running to the roar, for by doing so we may not only lessen the sting of pain, but we may also learn from it the compassion that makes it possible to accompany others in their darkest hours.

# SIX

# Our Soul Is None of Our Business

*We dance round in a ring and suppose.*
*But the Secret sits in the middle and knows.*
— ROBERT FROST

**T**HERE HAVE BEEN TIMES IN **MY LIFE WHEN DESPITE MY SINCERITY AND DESIRE TO BE HELPFUL,** I have asked too many questions of another. Sometimes out of curiosity, but mostly out of genuine concern, I have, without knowing it or wanting to, delved too close to the sensitive centre to which only a few trusted people are allowed access. There have been times when I have ventured into territory that was none of my business, and I was told so.

There are some aspects of everyone's life that are truly off limits. There are dimensions of thought, feeling, and experience that are private and need to be kept so until a person is ready to entrust them to another. As a priest, chaplain, counsellor, and spiritual director, I have been privy to the self-disclosure of many people. I have heard numerous dark secrets, real and imagined fears, and delicate hopes. I have always felt privileged when this happens; it is a great honour to be welcomed into the inner sanctum of another's soul. But strangely enough, I have come to realize that our own soul is none of our business!

## SOUL IS THE CENTRE OF THE CIRCLE

Because it lacks material concreteness, soul is difficult to define. The word does not denote something inside us, but the sacred depths *of* us. By soul I mean that dimension of our being that is like the eye of a hurricane. It is the still, quiet centre that lies hidden within the swirl of life's complexity. Soul is that sacred aspect of us referred to by the Taoist Chuang Tzu who states, "When we understand, we are at the centre of the circle and there we sit while 'Yes' and 'No' chase each other around the circumference."[1] Robert Frost refers to the same reality when he says, "We dance round in a ring and suppose. But the Secret sits in the middle and knows."[2]

We are not usually aware of our soul-self until we lose touch with it and experience ourselves adrift from our own life and out of sync with others, as the following story illustrates. A group of men earned their livelihood as porters. Tourists hired the porters to carry their supplies while on a safari. During the long, hot trek into the jungle, they suddenly stopped, set down their burden and refused to take another step. When asked why they had done so, one replied, "We can't go on; we have to wait for our souls to catch up to us."

When for long periods we carry burdens – be they physical, mental, or emotional – we become worn out, stressed out, and/or burnt out. Any one of these states can render us incapable of going on, unable to function, and wondering why we remain in work situations or personal relationships that are depleting. In any case, when we lay down our burdens, when we give ourselves a break, when we let our souls catch up to us, we can feel ourselves coming alive. Soul may be more difficult to grasp than the other aspects of our being, but it is no less real.

## EGO WANTS TO RUN THE SHOW

I hope you realize that I'm serious when I say our soul is none of our business, but I also hope it's clear that I don't mean it literally. Of course we must take responsibility for our soul's well-being, just as we do for our physical, mental, and emotional health. We can and should take the steps necessary to feed our soul. Meditation, journalling, spiritual direction, retreats, spiritual reading, venturing into nature, listening to soothing music, and even our hobbies can help us connect with our deep-self. By means of activities of this sort, we cultivate a way of being fully present to the moment, and thus poised to be smitten by the extraordinary nature of ordinary life. What is none of our business in this regard is the timing or outcome of our efforts.

There is a wise Buddhist dictum which says that enlightenment is an accident, and that a spiritual practice makes us accident prone. Whether or not we experience an accident – those sometimes dramatic, sometimes subtle aha moments when we sense the divinity of daily life, of nature, of another person, or of ourselves – whether we experience any of these is none of our business, but by faithfulness to our practices and by being fully present to the present, we put ourselves on a collision course with the sacred.

In my role as a spiritual director, I often find myself saying "it's none of your business" to people striving to deepen their sense of themselves as spiritual beings, to people who constantly try to discern whether they are making progress, or who want to know if the difficulties they are dealing with will change them for the better. These things are none of our business because the need to track our progress toward the attainment of spiritual goals is a function of the ego. And although our ego is an essential dimension of ourselves, one whose voice it may be good to heed in practical matters, if we continually bow to its demands to take control of our soul, it inhibits the process of spiritual growth. The vitality of the soul involves letting go, surrendering, yielding, entrusting ourselves to an inner wisdom that is other than that of our conscious, ego self.

Despite the fact that the soul is none of its business, our ego is nosey; it wants to know and dictate the when, where, why, and how of our soul's life. Our self-conscious self wants to run the show. But no matter how well-intentioned we may be, if we cede power to our ego in this regard, we end up getting in our own way. This is the point of the story about a student who approached the master saying, "How long will it take me to reach enlightenment?"

The master replied, "Five years."

The student, frustrated by what seemed like an eternity and desiring to attain his goal more quickly, said in response, "What if I try hard?"

The master in his wisdom simply replied, "Ten years!"

Ego wants to achieve enlightenment yesterday.

## CHANGE VERSUS TRANSFORMATION

Perhaps a way to help clarify the wisdom of resisting the ego's need to take over the life of our soul is to consider the difference between change and transformation. Change, whether in a corporation, a family, or in our individual lives, is something we make happen by exerting effort, by mustering our forces physically, mentally, emotionally, or in all these ways. We make plans, set goals, and chart the course for change. And as we move along in this process we analyze, measure, and when necessary re-evaluate our strategies. Change is an accomplishment brought about by the ego's efforts.

Transformation is another story. In Greek, the word for soul and butterfly is the same – *psyche*. When we speak of the metamorphosis wherein a caterpillar becomes a butterfly, we do not say that the caterpillar changed itself. Rather, subject to the laws of its nature, it is transformed. The caterpillar does not do anything to itself; rather, it simply yields to nature's way and becomes a new reality.

Similarly, despite the importance of faithfulness to a spiritual practice, it is not just showing up that issues in our transformation, for we must yield, trust, let go, and be open to the spiritual forces that are at work within us. How transformation actually takes place, the amount of time it requires, the unforeseen events that may impact it, and everything else related to it, including what we will look like when it's over – if it ever is over – is none of our business.

Change, it has been said, is the only constant in life; nothing remains the same for long. Change is an ongoing process that is often stressful because it disrupts our comfortable, or at least our familiar, routines. Transformation, though often undetectable, is also ongoing. And like change, transformation can also be difficult, not because it disrupts our *way* of life, but because it disrupts our *very* life; that is, our identity, our self-understanding, our sense of who we are.

The transformation that is none of our business is a process that issues in the death of the self we thought we were. As we open ourselves to life's lessons and to the impact that comes with faithfulness to a spiritual practice, we find that our sense of who we are becomes less concrete. Slowly, gradually, imperceptibly, we become more butterfly-like, more soulfully present and responsive to life, and less inclined to manipulate it. We are no longer just our ego, the self we have known our self to be, for we become a Self we do not know. This transformation is, perhaps, what St. Paul experienced when he stated, "it is no longer I who live, but it is Christ who lives in me" (Galatians 2:20).

## THE SELF WE DO NOT KNOW

The "new person" that transformation brings about, the self we do not know, is the Self we come to know (become one with) in silence. Commenting on Thomas Merton's poem *In Silence*, Roger Housden says this.

*In this depth of silence, the question Who are you? is likely to emerge ... Can we dare to hold the question, to feel the force that the words contain, without leaping to diffuse its potency with a clever answer? As we rest deeper into the silence that is at the heart of everything, we are able to rest in who we are beyond all thought and reason. We are able to be the one we do not know.*[3]

Talk about scary. To go with the flow of transformation is like disappearing before our very eyes. Because it is a matter of its life and death, our ego will resist this demise as surely as we would grasp for a branch if we were to fall off a cliff. It's a good thing spiritual growth is none of our business, because if it was, it might never happen.

It is no wonder so many of us avoid the void of silence, for although it is the "place" where we find the treasure of our True Self, it is also where happens the frightening experience of the passing away of the person we've known ourselves to be.

It is difficult to yield, to let go, to trust, and to entrust ourselves to forces we cannot comprehend, yet doing so is very freeing. Not having done it myself, I can only imagine how scary it must be to jump from an airplane for the first time. But what brings people to that experience over and over again is the exhilaration of the free fall. When we do not make the process or the outcome of spiritual growth our ego's business, there is a freedom, an exhilaration, a liberation from self pre-occupation that is its own reward.

While making a retreat at Genesee Abbey, I spoke with a monk who embodied the freedom from self pre-occupation just referred to. I asked him whether he experienced God's presence more now than he did 30 years ago when he entered the monastery. Fully expecting him to say "yes," I was taken aback *not* when he responded "no," but by the words he uttered next, which were "but now it doesn't matter." (He might just as well have said, "Who cares?") This is the voice of one who has not allowed his spiritual life to become his ego's business. Now the life of his soul was not a matter of feelings, but of faith.

## LANDING IN A FIELD OF DREAMS

Like a parachutist, there is a leap required if we are to experience the freedom that comes with leaving our ego behind. But if we take that leap, if we do not let our soul become our ego's business, we may find that when we hit the ground, we land in the field Rumi speaks of in his poem "A Great Wagon."

> *Out beyond ideas of wrong-doing and right-doing,*
> *There is a field. I'll meet you there.*
> *When the soul lies down in that grass*
> *The world is too full to talk about.*
> *Ideas, language, even the phrase "each other"*
> *Doesn't make any sense.*[4]

When we are taken up with ideas of "wrong-doing and right-doing," when "yes" and "no" chase one another in our heads, when we "dance round in a ring and suppose," we are in the life that is our business. Here we are in the world of "each other," the practical world of dualism where we exist as people separate from one another; this is what many call "the real world." But there is another world, and a larger life that is both within and beyond us – it is a "field of dreams" where we are one with ourselves, others, creation, and the God of our understanding.

Rumi's field is our spiritual home; it is the "centre of the circle," the Secret that "sits in the middle and knows," the "grass" upon which we are called to lie down together and rest, and from which we are summoned to transform the "real world" into the "Kin-dom" (web of loving relationships) it is meant to be. Rumi's field is more real than the "real world," for it is heaven on earth.

# CONTEMPLATION AND ENTRAINMENT

Even though, as Rumi states, language doesn't make any sense in this place of union, there are two words that are relevant to our connection with that larger life: contemplation and entrainment. Contemplation is from the Latin *con templari* and, according to spiritual teacher Brother David Steindl-Rast, *templari* refers to an area of the sky upon which seers fix their gaze in order to determine the immutable order according to which matters below are to be arranged. Living contemplatively, then, is not a matter of sequestering ourselves, or merely gazing at the heavens, but of living in harmony with the universal order. Contemplation requires sensitivity to the spiritual force that moves the stars because it is a living template for how our individual and collective lives are best lived on earth – as above, so below. About that force it has been said *ordo est amor*, "the order is love."

Entrainment refers to the phenomenon that can be observed when two rhythmic objects – clocks with pendulums, for instance – are in close proximity. What will happen is that their separate pendulums will eventually become locked in the same pattern of movement. We are influenced by that to which we are in proximity. For our purposes, entrainment has to do with the presence of a reality with which we are meant to live in harmony. Our individual souls are entrained to life's soul. This is none of our business, meaning we don't *make* this harmony happen, but what we *can* do is be willing to sense a greater Presence and surrender to its influence.

## IN SYNC AND OUT OF STEP

We live in response to the sacred when we take responsibility for the life of our soul. By being faithful to a spiritual practice, and by not allowing our soul to become our ego's business, we take a liberating leap into a self we do not know. This free fall enables us to become accident prone, poised to experience the sacred depths of ordinary life. When what we want to see is the quick results of change, it is difficult to accept the slow unfolding of transformation that is necessary if we are to become our soul-self. But to live contemplatively and to be entrained to the spiritual forces at play in nature and in human nature is the way of wisdom which, like all matters of the soul, is none of our business.

# SEVEN

# Whatever Is Happening Should Be Happening

*Life is what happens while you're busy
making other plans.*
— JOHN LENNON

I DON'T RECALL WHEN I FIRST HEARD THE STATEMENT "WHATEVER IS HAPPENING SHOULD BE HAPPENING," BUT I HAVE REPEATED IT MORE TIMES THAN I CAN COUNT. I find this notion comforting, especially when what is happening in my life is other than what I prefer. It helps me to be open to the possibility that there is a wisdom at play in the universe when I can find a conceptual place to put life's unfairness, randomness, and inconsistency. I may not know the whys and wherefores, but when I trust that life is unfolding as it ought to my own life unfolds more gracefully.

I must admit that many of the people with whom I have shared this statement have not embraced it as readily as I have; the word *should*, I believe, is the reason for their reluctance. *Should* seems to imply a rightness that precludes question; it appears to say that nothing else is supposed to be happening except that which is happening, and that what is happening is the best of all possibilities. I don't believe war is better than peace, or a pandemic is preferable to health. I don't believe that a world endangered by global warming and where poverty, hunger, and homelessness are all too prevalent should be accepted without an effort to change these harsh realities. *Should* does not preclude *could*; it is not resignation, but a prelude to possibility.

I don't know who spoke or wrote these simple words, but they strike me as profoundly true:"Happiness is found not in erasing, but embracing." Another wise dictum is the radical phrase *amor fati*,"love your fate"; both of these statements challenge us to put our arms around the reality of whatever is happening. When we truly accept what is happening, when we refuse to expend time and energy bemoaning what we wish was different, we are better positioned to bring about whatever changes might be necessary in order to make the world a better place.

## OBEYING LIFE

It was a crisp autumn morning when, while running through a park near my house, I encountered a man walking his dog. He had stopped and was training the dog to sit, heel, and retrieve a ball. The dog was doing everything its owner commanded and as I passed by I commented, "Would that life was that obedient." One-upping my best attempt at wisdom, the man replied, "Sometimes we have to obey life."

Obeying life – now there's an interesting concept, and a difficult task. Life can at times be wonderful and rewarding, but it is often unpredictable, unfair, demanding, scary, and all kinds of things that feel just plain "wrong." But life is what life is and I have two options in the face of that fact – take it or leave it.

As a child, I would often come home from school hungry and ask my mother, "What's for dinner?" She would sometimes respond, "You can have stew, or nothing!" There are times when I would rather have nothing than have what I don't want. I would rather sit and stew than eat stew – it's the one-piece puzzle thing. But stew is nourishing whether I like it or not, and so is facing into whatever is happening.

When we fully accept whatever is happening, we live in obedience to life. The word obey is derived from the Latin *audiere*, which means to listen. Obeying life means respectfully listening to people, situations, and circumstances, and responding to them in responsible and loving ways. If we accept the fact that whatever is happening should be happening, we won't, for instance, waste time wishing the people we are with were not there, or that they were different than they are. Instead, we will encounter them as if no one else was in the room. We may not find people any more interesting for doing this, but we might come to recognize their innate dignity. This was a lesson child psychiatrist Robert Coles learned and wrote about in his biography of Dorothy Day.

Throughout the mid-20th century, Day, the founder of the Catholic Worker Movement, was a champion of the poor, homeless, and unemployed in the Bowery district of Manhattan and beyond. Coles, a medical student in New York when he heard about Day's work, set out to meet her. When he located the Catholic Worker house, he entered the building and here describes what he encountered.

*She [Day] was sitting at a table, talking with a woman who was, I quickly realized, quite drunk, yet determined to carry on a conversation ...*

*I found myself increasingly confused by what seemed to be an interminable, essentially absurd exchange taking place between the two middle-aged women. When would it end – the alcoholic ranting and the silent nodding ... Finally, silence fell upon the room.*

*Dorothy Day asked the woman if she would mind an interruption. She got up and came over to me. She said, "Are you waiting to talk with one of us?"[1]*

Commenting on her question, Coles states that he found the words "with one of us" life-changing. The words were a statement of radical equality, one that went beyond the external criterion by which we generally judge acceptability and worth. Every person, no matter what their condition or circumstance, is valuable and worthy of our full attention and respect. It would be outrageous to say the woman Day was speaking with *should* be drunk, as if being inebriated was preferable to being sober, but Day seemed to fully accept what was happening, for she listened intently to the woman and responded in a reverent manner.

## BOREDOM IS MY FAULT

Upon first reading Cole's description of this encounter, I thought surely Day must have been bored by the woman with whom she was speaking, but I thought otherwise when I heard this definition: boredom is the decision (usually unconscious) that the present moment or person is not worth our full attention. I had always assumed that when I was bored it was the fault of the people I was with, the work

I was doing, or a lack of interesting activity. It had never dawned on me that I might be the cause of my boredom.

There is, of course, such a thing as a boring person – someone who, for example, doesn't know when to stop talking about things that are of no interest to you. Some forms of work can be boring in that they require physical or mental repetition. And the absence of activities that stimulate us does tend to have a deadening effect on our psyche. But I have come to realize that even situations like these don't have to be as boring as they may seem. Accepting that whatever is happening should be happening, and choosing to attend more fully to what is before me, can transform a tedious experience into one that is at least quasi-interesting.

Along with writing this book, one of the things before me is the work involved in preparing a religion class I will be teaching at Colorado College. I enjoy challenging students to grapple with ideas that have the potential to open their minds and hearts, but I find it difficult to create a syllabus and to map out goals and learning objectives. I have to remind myself continually that the effort is worth it, and I have to resist my impulse to procrastinate and to fall prey to the allure of a thousand distractions. But most of all I have to get in touch with why I agreed to teach in the first place, and with the fact that in the process of preparation I can learn more about a subject that is close to my heart. When I connect with what motivates me, the process of preparation becomes more enjoyable and less boring, and I find myself enlivened rather than drained.

When I open myself to the truth that whatever is happening should be happening, I am less likely to miss the full significance of those activities that are a necessary means to the attainment of my goals. Rehearsing for a performance, practicing for a game, studying for an exam – all these activities, and the time required to do them, are life happening, and they can be satisfying if I give myself to them as fully as I intend to give myself to that for which they are a preparation.

## INTERRUPTIONS, CONTROL, AND SCRIPTS

Charles Dickens' *A Tale of Two Cities* was written about London and Paris during the time of the French Revolution (1789–1799), but this classic novel is also about the way things are now, will be, and have always been. Every era is the best of times and the worst of times. Every age is a tale of victory and defeat– social, political, and religious. And in every person's life there are times of joy and sorrow – personal, professional, and relational. This being the case, it seems a bit petty to complain about interruptions, but it is most often these small, daily interferences with my plans that are the things I wish weren't happening. I wish war, tsunamis, gang violence, and genocide weren't happening, but they are not happening to *me*. When I own my reaction to the events in my life without judging their significance in comparison to bigger problems and less fortunate people, I have to admit to being frustrated by interruptions.

Is there ever a day, or a life, that goes by without interruption? Because the answer to this question is always "no," it is essential that we learn to recognize the unforeseen and unwelcome circumstances of life as things that should be happening; if we do not accept them as such and learn what they have to teach, we will be at odds with all that is beyond our control – which is pretty much everyone and everything – and we will live as if life was our adversary.

The desire to control life is as close to universal as anything I have discovered in the human race. It is as if we write a script in our heads for how a specific event or relationship should unfold. We write it for today, for tomorrow, and for a lifetime; we even write it for others so that their part in the play will mesh well with our own role. By our script, or at least by mine, life should occur without a hitch; no surprises, no accidents, no trials or tragedies – and no interruptions.

Plays, films, and other scripted events stay close to what is written, but life does not. Perhaps there is a script other than ours to which life is faithful, but its various scenes almost always stray from my idea of what should happen. You may have heard the saying that the only difference between stumbling blocks and building blocks is the way we use them. What I view as troublesome or problematic may actually be so only because I choose to see it that way. But if I accept the possibility that life is following a script other than my own, I might then engage in what I find troublesome rather than rail against it; I can choose to loosen my grip on the need to control, and I can discover new and life-giving paths I had never imagined.

I don't know a single alcoholic who wrote that part into their life's script. But I know many who have embraced the fact of their alcoholism and are now helping others who struggle with that addiction. Likewise, I don't know anyone who planned to have cancer, but I know a number of cancer survivors who now live every day of their lives gratefully, and who counsel others to do the same. These are but two of the many ways we can turn personal tragedies into triumphs, two examples of how stumbling blocks can become building blocks that make of our lives an enduring edifice.

## TIME AND KNOWING WHY

One of the things that make it difficult for me to embrace whatever is happening has to do with time and how there never seems to be enough of it. "I don't have time for this aggravation." "I don't have time to clean up the mess you've made." "I don't have time for this heart attack!" Because our lives are often overfull and all of our time is accounted for, many of the things that happen are hard to embrace; they take time we don't have.

I have found it helpful not to consider time quantitatively; that is, not as something I have more or less of but, instead, to think of it qualitatively, as when someone, after having an uplifting experience, might say, "I had the time of my life." Every day is the time of our life. Every day is the only day we have to live. Yes, time is quantifiable and can be divided into seconds, minutes, and hours, days, months, and years, but we can also relate to it as an opportunity to live and to give our all to everyone we encounter, to everything we experience – to whatever is happening.

Another reason I fail to live fully and to accept whatever is happening is that I want to know *why* it's happening; I want reasons and answers. I know I'm not alone in my need for explanations. Dani has had many misfortunes come her way in the past few years; she has been diagnosed with bipolar disease, her husband left her, she lives close to the poverty line, and she is trying unsuccessfully to get her children to tolerate one another. By the time she revealed all of this to me, Dani had come upon a pretty good way to deal with her life, but still found herself asking, "why?"

Dani is a Buddhist, so instead of getting angry at God, which is what she did as a Catholic, she now gets curious. Her question has shifted from, "Why is this happening to me?" spoken while shaking a clenched fist at the sky, to a statement better understood as "I *wonder* why this is happening *for* me?" When we wonder at the things that befall us, we aren't so much looking for reasons or answers, as we are opening ourselves to life's wisdom. Wonder and wisdom imply the willingness to be taught life's lessons, like them or not, ready or not.

When we resist what is happening and when we insist on answers that will satisfy our need to know "why," we are like a child trying to protect her or his newly erected sandcastle from an oncoming wave. Everything we have and everyone – ourselves included – that is a part of our life is as vulnerable as a sandcastle on the seashore. Not every wave reaches far enough to undo what we have created or what we value, but every once in a while, in the midst of the many good things that happen, we are left in ruins. I wonder why?

In light of our vulnerability and impermanence on this earth, I find the following description of Sufism a good way to approach life and to deal with the reality of whatever is happening: "Whatever you have in your mind – forget it. Whatever you have in your hand – give it. Whatever is to be your fate – face it." When we engage the reality of our lives with a detached, generous, and open-to-the-present attitude, whatever is happening, even when it is difficult or hurtful, becomes a reality with which we can cope and through which we can grow.

## IN SYNC AND OUT OF STEP

In order to embrace the wisdom of "whatever is happening should be happening," we have to be willing to listen and to respond to the sacred. Conventional wisdom tells us to resist what we think isn't right or what we don't like. Although this is often a good and even necessary approach to life, if we do not first accept what is happening, we may find ourselves at odds with life much of the time. When we realize we must obey life rather than do battle with it, when we learn to pay attention to the things, the people, and the interruptions that make up our day rather than resist and resent them, we are better positioned to change what must be changed, and to wonder "why" rather than ask "why me?"

# EIGHT

# The Virtue of Half-Hearted Commitment

*Memento mori, memento vivere.*
*"Remember death, remember to live."*
— UNKNOWN

**F**OR MANY PEOPLE, COMMIT-
MENT IS ONE OF THE SCARIEST WORDS IN OUR VOCABU-
LARY. The idea of choosing something or someone in a way
that excludes other possibilities can feel limiting or even
suffocating. Commitment closes doors and forces us to nar-
row our scope.

On the other hand, commitment can be liberating. To
have identified something or someone that will be the pri-
mary focus of our time and energy can free us from indeci-
sion and enable us to unleash the full force of our creativity
and passion.

For a period of four years, I served on the staff of a no-
vitiate, a monastic setting where those seeking acceptance

into a religious order spend a year in a life of prayer, silence, and manual labour. The schedule was tight, the distractions were few, and the limits on leaving the premises were strict. The purpose of the year and of the rules was to give the novices ample opportunity to get to know themselves so they could make a decision about whether to take temporary vows of poverty, celibacy, and obedience at the conclusion of the year.

Religious and marital vows are a form of commitment that can be both limiting and liberating. To choose either way of life precludes other options, but by choosing one or the other, a person can realize their full potential as a human being. The same is true for other forms of commitment. I am in awe of the dedication required to reach one's potential as an artist, musician, or professional or Olympic athlete. The women and men who follow these paths must say a resolute "no" to other opportunities and constant distractions. They must discipline themselves to endure many setbacks and frustrations, but, in the end, they excel at what they do in a way that could never happen without a total commitment to the process.

## HALF-HEARTEDLY COMMITTED, WHOLEHEARTEDLY INVOLVED

Given the fact that commitment is necessary in order to do and to become our best, how can it be virtuous to be half-hearted? How can it be a good thing to be committed conditionally? In order to fathom this conundrum, I will refer to what a psychologist-friend shared with me years ago. Quoting a study he had read, Dick explained that there are a variety of combinations having to do with commitment and involvement. A person can be

*half-heartedly committed and half-heartedly involved*
*wholeheartedly committed and wholeheartedly involved*
*half-heartedly committed and wholeheartedly involved*
*wholeheartedly committed and half-heartedly involved*

It would seem, Dick claimed, that the best combination of commitment and involvement, the most advantageous way to live, is to be wholeheartedly committed and wholeheartedly involved, but this, he said, is the definition of a fanatic.

Fanatical people can be fun to watch, for they are without the inhibitions that shackle most of us. If you don't believe me, just observe the crowd at a professional hockey game! But it is also true that fanatical people can be difficult to deal with, for in their exuberant behaviour and unquestioned loyalty to a team, a cause, or a person, they can lack objectivity and sensibility. Those who approach life both wholeheartedly committed and wholeheartedly involved often fail to listen to the voice of reason and they sometimes act in ways that are offensive.

As we pondered commitment and involvement, both Dick and I agreed that the best way to engage life is also the most difficult; namely, to be half-heartedly committed but wholeheartedly involved. Half-hearted commitment does not mean that a person is wishy-washy, or that she/he isn't fully convinced of the goodness or rightness of an organization, an endeavour, or a relationship; rather, half-heartedness refers to the willingness to see reality as it is. No institution, country, religion, corporation, or person is without shortcomings. No entity on this earth is flawless. This fact need not prevent us from involving and investing ourselves wholeheartedly in whatever we do, but it should make us aware of the importance of being objective and realistic, lest our enthusiasm prevent us from being appropriately critical.

## HEART OVER HEAD

Let's consider marriage as an illustration of the virtue of half-hearted commitment. Most relationships that lead to marriage begin with infatuation, that period of wholehearted commitment and involvement wherein the other person is thought to be god or goddess-like. Practically all of one's thoughts, feelings, and actions are centred on the one with whom we are smitten, and in whom we find no fault. Nothing is too good for the person we love, and no one is more attractive. This is not just a matter of being "head over heels," but "heart over head," for it is often while in this non-objective, less-than-sober, and delightfully irrational state that two people enter into the commitment of marriage.

The honeymoon phase of marriage can prolong their euphoria, the sense that each person is totally content with the other and with their life together, but eventually any one of a thousand things can happen that shatter the idyllic illusion of marriage as a happily-ever-after affair, and of one's partner as a person whose flaws, now evident, are charming! It is at this point that spouses sometimes begin to question their commitment. Did I make a mistake? Is my partner the person I thought she/he was? Should I look elsewhere for the person who will make me happy? Now the blinders are off. Now the other person is no longer on a pedestal. Now marriage can truly begin if the bottom line of trust and respect is intact. Not all couples should remain married, but those who experience disillusionment with their spouse are usually stronger for honestly acknowledging and gently communicating about their own and their partner's faults.

Half-heartedness in relation to commitment is about seeing reality with clear eyes; it is about acknowledging faults and embracing people, causes, and careers for who and what they are. It is more difficult to involve one's self wholeheartedly in someone or something that has lost its luster, but the willingness to do so is what virtue and maturity are all about. Most of the world's great sages and spiritual leaders teach that giving ourselves one hundred percent to life is what leads to happiness. This may be so, but what leads to integrity is the willingness to give our all, knowing that what or who we give ourselves to, though deserving of our whole-hearted involvement, may not be worthy of blind, uncritical commitment.

## LOVING OUR IMPERFECT SELVES

As I have said in my other books, I think it's important to acknowledge our faults and failings, but to love ourselves nonetheless. This is what half-hearted commitment and wholehearted involvement look like in relation to ourselves. Maturity demands that we take an honest inventory of our strengths and weaknesses, our virtues and vices, and, having done so, wholeheartedly accept the person we are, flaws included. Acceptance does not preclude attempts to grow beyond our faults, but it gives us the solid ground of self-love from which to operate. Conversely, if we allow the reality of our imperfections to prevent us from loving ourselves, we will not only tend to be overly self-critical, but we will likely be quick to cast a critical eye on others. As French-born writer Anaïs Nin has stated, "We don't see others as they are, we see them as we are."[1]

I was reminded of this while speaking with a directee who told me about his penchant for focusing on what is wrong with himself, others, and the world. While I believe it is important to see with sober eyes, I also know how easy it is to see with sombre eyes; that is, to see only what is wrong, or what needs improvement. This form of half-hearted commitment characterized by fault-finding, negativity, and pessimism is not a virtue, but a vice. Such a mindset is not a strength, but a weakness of character that serves only to promote a sense of inadequacy when we communicate it to ourselves in the form of negative self-talk, or to others as criticism and judgment.

As important as it is to accept and to love ourselves, if we do not recognize and admit our faults, we become prone to narcissism, a kind of self-fanaticism, one characteristic of which is to always see others as the cause of our problems, but never ourselves. Narcissus is the name of the Greek mythical figure who fell in love with his own reflection, but Narcissus has many names today. One of those names is Ken, a man whose wife discovered after ten years of marriage that he was a sex addict. Ken's addiction led him not only into a number of extra-marital relationships, but also into pornographic bookstores and other public places where he sometimes exposed himself. Despite the fact that his illness put both he and his family at risk in various ways, Ken never once apologized for his behaviour and, to this day, considers it his former wife's fault that their marriage ended in divorce. It is good to be a fan of oneself, but not a fanatic. It is painful to be in the presence of people who do not love themselves, but it is *a pain* to be with those who love themselves too much!

## HALF-HEARTED THINKING

Another problem with wholehearted commitment has to do with a way of thinking that is limited due to conclusions drawn from wrong assumptions. Perhaps a mundane example will help to clarify what I mean. Some time ago while I was visiting my mother, we took her car to run some errands. Returning to the car after several hours, I noticed that the driver's side door was ajar. I immediately concluded that because the interior light would have remained on during our absence, the battery was probably dead. In fact, when I attempted to start the car the engine would not turn over. We waited an hour for road service, and paid close to $50 at a repair shop the next day, only to find out that the car wouldn't start because I failed to turn off the "kill switch," a theft prevention device I had engaged when we left the car. In a sense, I had become so wholeheartedly committed to a way of thinking about the situation that I failed to consider other possibilities as the cause of the problem.

Conviction about our beliefs and opinions can be empowering; being certain about what we think and how we feel gives us a sense of confidence and assurance. But it is sometimes the case that in our interactions with others, wholehearted commitment to our convictions can lead to an unwillingness to see a bigger picture, to our becoming close-minded, and to losing the capacity for listening and empathy. Rigidity, righteousness, and fundamentalism are born of wholehearted commitment, a verity that is often evident in those whose religious beliefs are based on a literal reading of scripture. Without the openness that characterizes half-hearted commitment, limited thinking can lead to arguments interpersonally. Internationally, it often lays the groundwork for wars.

## SEEING CLEARLY, ACTING BOLDLY

A person who is half-heartedly committed and wholeheartedly involved is a valuable asset in any relationship or endeavour, be it personal or professional. Such a person is willing and able not only to see what is wrong, missing, or in need of improvement, but also able to give voice to what she/he has identified as problematic. Someone who is both wholeheartedly committed and wholeheartedly involved might, because of their enthusiasm, not see clearly what needs to be corrected. One who is both half-heartedly committed and half-heartedly involved might not be willing to address a problem even if it was noticed. But the one who both sees and cares enough to act can be a catalyst for change and growth.

As an illustration of this, I think of Rosa Parks, the African-American woman whom many view as having set the civil rights movement in motion. Rosa was willing to see that the mistreatment of blacks and other minorities, though allowed by the law of the land, was wrong. She became wholeheartedly involved in correcting this wrong when she refused to sit at the back of a bus, the place assigned to blacks in the south and in other parts of the United States in the mid-20th century. I think, too, of the countless number of people who look with clear and caring eyes at their spouses, children, friends, and colleagues, and who risk misunderstanding, rejection, and ridicule when, motivated by a desire for the good of the other – the family, the corporation, or society in general – give honest feedback and take necessary action.

# REMEMBER DEATH, REMEMBER TO LIVE

It occurs to me that the ultimate challenge of the virtue of half-hearted commitment has to do with death. Despite knowing that death is inevitable, many of us walk the earth as if we will walk it forever. We give little or no thought to the fact that all we have we will *not* have, and that who we are will cease to be. I am all for the power of positive thinking, and I know too well the limiting effect of a sombre outlook, but I believe the reluctance to look death in the face makes it impossible to live life to the full.

In his Pulitzer Prize-winning book *The Denial of Death*, cultural anthropologist Ernest Becker claims that all of our efforts to be "somebody," everything from heroic acts to the accumulation of wealth and power, stem from our fear of death. In other words, we become fanatical about life when our fear of death results in a refusal to be influenced by its inevitability and finality. But if we are half-heartedly committed to life, we open ourselves to the truth that life in general and our life in particular are both fragile and finite. When we accept this reality but do not allow it to prevent us from wholehearted involvement, we live every day not with a desperate desire to squeeze the life out of it, but with a passionate, grateful, and reverent willingness to taste its bittersweetness.

*Memento mori, memento vivere*, is Latin for "remember death, remember to live." This is surely a saying worth pondering, and one that supports the virtue and wisdom of being half-heartedly committed but wholeheartedly involved.

## IN SYNC AND OUT OF STEP

It is the voice of the sacred that calls us beyond the fanaticism of wholehearted commitment and involvement. Although it can be exhilarating to be "heart over head," and despite the fact that willingness to see the flaws in a person, a movement, or an organization may make it more difficult to be wholeheartedly involved with them, to close our eyes to the imperfection of reality is not a virtue. Authenticity and integrity require the courage to keep our mind and heart open to the value and beauty of that which is imperfect and, despite the strength of our convictions, to listen deeply to the opinion of others. Because everyone and everything will one day cease to be, living in sync with the sacred invites us to *memento vivere, to live* wholeheartedly.

# NINE

# We Are More Than Our Limp

*Jesus is the only son of God, and so am I and so are you.*
— WILLIAM BLAKE

IN HIS CD SERIES *MERTON'S PATH TO THE PALACE OF NOWHERE*, FORMER MONK AND PSYCHOLOGIST JAMES FINLEY SPEAKS ABOUT THE DIF-FERENCE BETWEEN SPIRITUAL MASTERS AND THE REST OF US. Finley claims that spiritual masters are not without their flaws and, using physical disability as a metaphor, he states that "the master limps." More to the point, Finley claims that masters, unlike most people, are not handicapped by their limping because they know their limp doesn't have the power to name who they are. Knowing that they are more than their limp, masters do not identify with their limp. Rather, they merely see themselves as someone who happens to be flawed like everyone else. Masters are also afraid, Finley says, but not frightened by their fear; and although they can become confused, they are not confused by their confusion.

For most of us, fear is frightening, and confusion is confusing. When I am confused or uncertain about something, by definition, I lack clarity. In the realm of our logical, day-to-day living, confusion is problematic. Confusion makes it difficult to solve problems, to negotiate the labyrinthine ways of relationships, to competently perform our tasks at work, and to get from one end of the day to the other safely and constructively. It is a good thing when we are not confused.

In the intricacies of the spiritual life, confusion refers to the state of being out of touch with our soul, that which has been called "the elusive essence of a thing." Soul is like the underbelly of an iceberg, the vast, unseen dimension of which our ego, or conscious self, is the visible tip. When we are confused, we don't realize that we are more than the peripheral ways we define ourselves. We are more than our personality traits and idiosyncrasies; we are more than our titles and roles, our physical appearance, mental capacity, and emotional ups and downs. If we are not vigilant, our confusion can confuse us and our ego can begin to dictate our identity.

## HONOURING THE NON-SENSE OF SOUL

Although they limp like the rest of us, spiritual masters are not handicapped by their limp, frightened by their fear, or confused by their confusion, because they are convinced beyond thought or feeling that they are more than their flaws; they realize that there is something sacred about them. It need not be a problem that we stumble through life with a limp – so what, "who cares?" We are closer to the only truth that matters when we know that our fears and confusion don't have the power to name who we are, and when we allow ourselves to rest and to revel in our soul – that dimension of ourselves that is other than our flawed self.

When speaking about such a thing as soul, or better, such a non-thing as soul, no words are adequate and no concepts are accurate. Here we are in the realm of the mysterious where oxymoron, contradiction, and paradox, rather than logic, reason, and orthodoxy are what make sense in a nonsensical way. In the life of the soul, to succeed may be to fail, to not know is wisdom, weakness may be strength, and dying to our ego is the way to fullness of life. When confronted by such paradoxical notions, I am tempted to plant my feet firmly on the ground and to pose cynical questions like the ones comedian Woody Allen asked about heaven: "How far is it from midtown, and can you get change for a twenty there?" Regarding the existence of the soul, the question might be, "Can it speak, and if so, will it whisper the winning lottery numbers in my ear?" In the end, though, it is best to give up both cynicism and the quest for clarity and, instead, embrace Rumi's good advice: "Sell your cleverness, and purchase bewilderment."

Although I know bewilderment is the better approach when dealing with paradoxical notions, the other thing I tend to do when I've reached my wit's end is to reach a little further; that is, to think a little harder. I even do this in matters of the heart where I know I'm not likely to reach clarity with my mind. Some years ago, I was introduced to and asked to give shelter to a man who was on the run from the Mafia. Salvatore knew enough to send his *capo*, his "boss," to prison, and he had seen enough to turn his stomach. He wanted out; the mob wanted him dead. Because Sal was the most street-smart and people-wise person I had ever met, I trusted his advice when, after telling him about a relationship I was grappling with, he simply said, "Think long, think wrong."

In most realms of life, thinking long and hard can be helpful, but when it comes to the unfathomable territory of the heart and soul, our head can lead us astray. I put Sal on a bus to Mexico a few days after our conversation and have never heard from him since. Thanks, Sal, wherever you are.

## EVERYTHING IS MORE THAN IT APPEARS

From the paradoxical perspective of the soul, it is possible to understand everything and everyone as being both down-to-earth and out-of-this-world at the same time. There is a concrete immediacy to all creation, a tangible materiality that is evident to our senses. When we look at someone or something, we see their physical being, but when we behold rather than look, when we gaze rather than glance, it becomes possible to penetrate beneath the surface to the boundless spiritual essence that both underlies and transcends them. This, I think, is what poet and mystic William Blake was referring to when he wrote, "If the doors of perception were cleansed everything would appear to man as it is: infinite."[1]

When speaking of this truth, devotees of Zen say, "First a mountain is a mountain. Then it is not a mountain. Then it is a mountain again." I have already stated that I live in the shadow of a mountain. When I look at Pike's Peak, I see a mountain consisting of earth, rock, and vegetation. But when I gaze through the eyes of my soul, the real becomes surreal. Now the mountain, while remaining a mountain, is somehow more than the sum of its parts. This insight is fleeting and when it departs I am left looking at a mountain again, though now with an appreciation for the mystery that is the essence of every mountain. Of course, in these changes of perspective, nothing has happened to the mountain, but something profound has happened to me, for I have now experienced the truth that not only mountains but all things and all people are more than they appear at first sight.

The realization that everything and everyone is more than meets the eye is perhaps most important in the realm of relationships. We may know someone for decades, but then be smitten by an awareness of them that pulls the rug out from under our sense of who they are. It is at this point that we are closer to knowing the full truth about that person, because we are all more than physical, mental, and emotional beings. In the depths of our souls we are a dimension of the universal Soul that pervades all of life. Pulizer Prize-winning author Annie Dillard gives voice to this truth when she writes, "Something pummels us, something barely sheathed. Power broods and lights. We are played on like a pipe; our breath is not our own."[2]

It takes a lifetime of practice, but bringing this depth of awareness to our relationships is what enables us to be a soulmate.

This insight into the spiritual essence of others is true of ourselves as well. At first sight we are who we know ourselves to be; we are what we think, feel, want, need, experience, and so on; we are our limp, our fears, and our confusion. But then, for no apparent reason, we may catch a glimpse of our true, sacred self, and although like the mountain we continue to be what we consist of – our imperfect, limping self – we suddenly know we are more, and in this knowing we are no longer frightened by our fears, or confused by our confusion. Perhaps you have had such an experience when looking in the mirror, or at a photograph of yourself, or seeing your name in print, and have wondered, "Is that me; am I that person?" Every now and then we can be surprised by the realization that we don't really know who we are, or that there is something about us we cannot fathom. These are mystical moments, religious experiences, instances of a holy befuddlement that invite us to see and embrace the truth that we are more than our limp, more than we appear even to ourselves. Though powerful, this awareness or experience is usually momentary, for we soon go back to living as if there is nothing more to us than we can see. The need to wake up is constant; the ability to stay awake is not.

## PRONE TO PROJECTION

If we are not aware of our own sacredness, we become prone to projection. That is, we start to see both positive and negative qualities in others that we don't recognize in ourselves. Negative projection takes place when we unconsciously assign to others those aspects of ourselves we deem unacceptable – fear, insecurity, pettiness, and the like.

Regarding positive projections, when we are in a dark place and go out into the bright sunlight, we literally cannot see what is before us. In a similar fashion, if we are "in the dark" about ourselves, it is possible to be so enamoured by the light of others that we see goodness, beauty, holiness, or wisdom in them, but are blind to those qualities in ourselves. This is a dynamic recognizable in many members of religious cults; the power of cult leaders is a reality not only because they may be charismatic, but also because their followers do not see their own depth, dignity, and divinity.

Positive projection of this sort may be a reality not only in cult-like groups on the fringe of the mainstream, but even in mainline religions. Christians, for instance, are taught that Jesus is God incarnate, but believing this is true only of him, they often overlook the divinity of their own humanity, limp and all. William Blake considered himself a Christian, but though he revered Jesus he was not blinded by his light, for it was he who said, "Jesus is the only son of God, and so am I, and so are you."[3] Affirming the paradoxical truth of Blake's statement is not a denial of Jesus' uniqueness, but an affirmation of what his body embodied – the godly nature of human nature, the divinity of all humanity. I realize this may sound heretical. If so, I hope that at least it is a "holy heresy," one that errs on the side of divinity's incarnate and benevolent nearness.

When we acknowledge the reality of our limp but resist the temptation to identify with it, we are like the master, be it Jesus, the Buddha, or any other spiritual figure. We don't hear much about it, but, being human, they too limped; they too had their share of fear, confusion, doubt, and the like. Masters, however, know that such feelings are just the tip of the iceberg.

## WEAKNESS CAN BE STRENGTH

Poet Rainer Maria Rilke, a master of sorts, knew that he limped. This is clear in a letter he wrote to an aspiring poet who sought his advice and counsel. Rilke knew the young man had put him on a pedestal, and he was anxious to let him know he didn't belong there.

*Do not believe that he who seeks to comfort you lives untroubled among the simple and quiet words that sometimes do you good. His life has much difficulty and sadness and remains far behind yours. Were it otherwise he would never have been able to find those words.*[4]

This statement is the testimony of someone who knew that he was more than his limp. When we allow our faults to "name who we are," we may feel that we have nothing to offer others; it may seem like we are depleted of strength, wisdom, insight, or anything else we might consider necessary in order to console or advise those in need. But when, like Rilke, we are not handicapped by our limp, we know our weakness can be a strength.

Because it gives me satisfaction to experience that my being "together" can be helpful to others, I would rather assist them from a place of strength and knowledge than from a place of woundedness; I would rather not be a "wounded healer." But I have found that in my moments of need what helps me most is not a fix for my problems, or answers to my questions, but the reassurance that having them is all right. And I am beginning to trust that identifying with and affirming another in their need is better in the long run than rescuing them, for when we are willing to share our fears and confusion with others rather than giving them pat answers to their dilemmas, they often discover within themselves the wisdom that helps them cope with life. Perhaps this is why psychoanalyst Carl Jung said that only the wounded physician heals.

## IN SYNC AND OUT OF STEP

When we embrace our limp but do not identify with it, we live in sync with the sacred. Then we do not spend time and energy trying to perfect ourselves or to attain some societal standard of acceptability. Instead, we stay focused on the deeper truth that who we are is a sacred Self. Then, too, there is no impulse to project, for we are in touch with the divinity of our humanity. And despite our flaws, we are not handicapped, frightened, confused, or any of the thousand other ways we can be tempted to think or feel that we are our limp. Having embraced our fears and confusion, we are better able to help others recognize that their handicaps do not have the power to name who they are.

# TEN

# Letting Go of an Offence Means Letting Go of the Self That Is Offended

*Forgiveness is the fragrance the violet
sheds on the heel that has crushed it.*

— MARK TWAIN

IT HAS BEEN SAID THAT THERE IS NO HOPE FOR A MARRIAGE WHERE THERE IS NO FORGIVENESS. The same applies to any significant relationship where there is a desire for growth and to overcome conflict and misunderstanding – whether that relationship is parent-child, employer-employee, friend-friend, nation-nation. The world works – when it does work – because people have found a way to forgive themselves and others for offences great and small, intended and unintended.

Offences come in many shapes and sizes; different things are offensive to different people. Some people, for example, are offended by crass language, some by being ignored, some by people who are pushy or arrogant, and others by those whose appearance is unkempt. Whatever the cause, the experience is the same; to be offended is to not have one's sense of fairness, appropriateness, or boundaries honoured.

Until I came across the statement that is the title of this chapter, I thought forgiveness meant excusing a person who offended me and going on as though nothing of a hurtful nature had happened between us. It wasn't exactly a "forgive and forget" approach since I rarely forget being hurt, but it *did* involve not letting the past interfere with the present or the future of a relationship. I now realize that true forgiveness has to do with something much more profound; forgiveness is about growing beyond, or beneath the ego, the part of me that "took the hit"; it's about opening myself to that aspect of my being that is my best self.

## GOING DEEPER

Because disappointing and hurtful occurrences are frequent, and because many of us are so prone to feeling them, learning to let go of the self that is offended is crucial. It reminds me of the *Far Side* greeting card that pictures two bears standing beside one another. One of them has a target on its chest and the other bear says to him, "Bummer of a birthmark, Hal!" Many of us are walking targets. We are super-sensitive. We are easily hurt.

I find it difficult to get through a day without something happening that leaves me feeling hurt, upset, or miffed in some manner. Depending on my mood, I can feel attacked, ignored, misunderstood, unappreciated, and sometimes all of those things, even when none of these reactions are appropriate to the situations that trigger them. But rather than attempting to develop "thick skin," or deflecting or denying what offends me, I am trying to look upon every offence as an invitation, an opportunity, a catalyst for growth, because I am convinced that the best approach to dealing with the reality of being offended is to embark on a spiritual journey, one that enables me to identify with and respond to life from a deeper place within myself – a place offences cannot reach.

Because my ego will always be with me, I expect to feel hurt to varying degrees my entire life; to be otherwise would mean I had become hardened and insensitive. However, as I grow to realize that I am more than my ego, and as I progress in the process of identifying with my soul and letting go of the self that is offended, I'm convinced that the offences I experience will wound me less severely, and that forgiveness will occur more readily. It was growth of this sort that enabled humorist and philosopher Mark Twain to say, "Forgiveness is the fragrance the violet sheds on the heel that has crushed it." When our ego takes its appropriate place in the backseat of our selves, it may become possible for forgiveness to emanate from us as naturally as does the aroma from a crushed flower.

## MOVING FROM EGO TO SOUL

According to Carl Jung, the purpose of life is to relocate the centre of gravity of the personality from the ego to the Self. This relocation is the spiritual journey I referred to above. Relocation is a life-long endeavour that requires dedication and discipline because our ego consists of those aspects of ourselves that we identify as being "us." Ego, to expand on philosopher René Descartes' infamous *cogito ergo sum*, "I think therefore I am," posits that we are what we think, feel, want, need, experience, and the like. Ego claims to be the totality of who we are. The soul, on the other hand, because it lacks concreteness, is less readily recognized as being a dimension of our self. This being the case, we must learn to be quiet and still in order to catch a glimpse, feel the stirrings, or hear the sounds of silence that arise from our deeper self.

If I were to attempt to draw a picture of my soul, there would be nothing visible on the paper. But if I attempted to *live* from my soul, you might observe a kind of aura that permeates my presence and actions. You might sense a quiet calm about me even though my life is filled with the chaos of conflicted relationships and deadlines too close to meet. You might also experience in me a deep joy that is unexplainably present despite the existence of painful losses. You might be baffled by my firmness and resolve as I voice an opinion that is unpopular, especially since you know it is hard for me to be the odd person out. And you might wonder out loud why I seem so nonplussed in the face of a derogatory comment that would wound the most callous among us.

This is what the soul looks like, or what it is like to live from it. This is the Self beneath the self we think we are. This is what we fall into when we let go of the self that is offended.

Because it is scary to let go of our ego and to cooperate with the relocation process Jung speaks about, we instinctively hold tight to our notion of our self even if we know that doing so prevents the possibility of being more calm, joyful, strong, and unruffled. But when we *do* let go of the self that is offended, it is not as if we cease to be who we've always been; it's just that we begin to open up to the fullness of who we are, and in that openness we glimpse the possibility of a new and richer life.

## DYING TO EGO

In "The Holy Longing," German poet Johann Wolfgang von Goethe speaks about letting go as a form of dying that issues in growth.

> *And so long as you haven't experienced*
> *this: to die and so to grow,*
> *you are only a troubled guest*
> *on the dark earth.*[1]

It is my experience that many of us try to make a home on this earth by clinging to our ego identity rather than by understanding ourselves in relation to our soul; we resist the dying and thereby forgo the growth about which Goethe writes. When we do this, trouble in the form of inner turmoil and darkness in the form of uncertainty is not far away.

Sharon is a woman of high principles. She is articulate about her values and stubborn in defence of them. At the beginning of our spiritual direction session, Sharon announced that she was experiencing a crisis. By this she meant that she had become someone she didn't like. Sharon had lost touch with the quiet centre of her soul and found herself at odds with almost everyone in her life. As we spoke, it became clear that she had so identified with her beliefs and values, that when others did not see life as she saw it, or did not agree with the conclusions she drew because of what she held dear, she felt angry, misunderstood, and unappreciated.

Sharon wanted to be compassionate, not intolerant. She wanted to be kind to others, not adversarial. But she wondered out loud, "Who am I if I let go of what I believe? How can I become the kind of person I want to be if I compromise my values?" Her dilemma was the beginning of a new phase of spiritual growth, an invitation to become a self she did not know.

It is scary to let go not only of the self that is offended but, as in Sharon's case, the self that offends. If we are to mature spiritually, we must let go not of our beliefs and values, but of the ego self that feels justified in clinging to them. What Sharon had to let go of was a tenacity born of righteousness, not the rightness of what she held to be true.

## BEYOND THE HORIZON OF OUR SELF

It has been said that the difference between a rut and a grave are the dimensions! A rut is not merely a pattern of behaviour that has become habitual and unrewarding, it can also be a way of thinking about ourselves that is limited, a view that stops at the horizon of what we have known and that fails to recognize the vast expanse that lies beyond.

The horizon where water meets sky is never more evident than at the ocean's edge. When we look into the distance, it is clear where the water and the sky touch one another, but the reality is that, despite its clarity from where we stand, they *never* touch. It is the same with us; who we are is different than who we appear to be. When we buy into the illusion that we are only who we think we are or who others want us to be, we stifle our soul, as Roger Housden states in a commentary on Rumi's poem "Unfold Your Own Life." In this excerpt, Housden calls these illusions about ourselves "stories."

*The [stories] that keep us treading water for thirty years without even noticing it until suddenly we have a bypass ... The stories in our head about what our parents thought we should be, about how inadequate we are, our lack of talent, or about how we were always destined for great things ...*

   *And don't be fooled by success stories either: by the wonderful business you have built or the books you have written ... They can seduce you ... and keep you running on the same wheel for the rest of your life without hearing even a whisper of a deeper sound, a sound inside you that has been singing since the day you were born.*[2]

If we never hear the sound of our soul inviting us beyond the horizon of who we think we are, the offences we experience will maintain their grip on us for a lifetime. We will ruminate about them and feed ourselves with tales about how unfairly we've been treated. It may in fact be the case that hurtful experiences were undeserved, but it is also true that we can fan the flame of our wounds into a roaring blaze.

   Confucius says that to be wronged is nothing unless we remember it. The self that is wronged is the self that remembers. Another saying of Chinese origins posits that they who are angry dig two graves. When we hold a grudge, we dig our own grave as well as that of the person(s) we despise. We lie confined in coffins of negativity, dark and lifeless states both emotionally and spiritually when we refuse to let go of our offended self.

## OFFENDING OUR SELF

The notion of letting go of the self that is offended applies not only when we are hurt by another, but also when our offences offend ourselves. Every one of us has done or said something we wish we hadn't, or failed to do or say something we wish we had. Each of us has wounded others in ways that have resulted in our feeling guilt, shame, remorse, or regret. "How could I have been so untrue to myself, so willing to compromise my values?" "Why did I not have the courage or awareness to make a better choice?"

Self-inflicted wounds are no less an invitation to let go of our ego than are offences caused by others, but I have found it more difficult to let go of the self that is offended when it is my own actions rather than someone else's that has caused me pain. When we do or say something we regret, we tend to hang around our ego, berating ourselves for falling short, for not being our ideal self. Although this leads nowhere, there is a payoff, for we can feel good about feeling bad. Even though we did something we consider wrong, at least we give ourselves a hard time for it! When we offend ourselves, what is called for is not self-criticism or blame, but the courage to admit to ourselves and, if appropriate, to a trusted other, what we are sorry for, and then to affirm that just as we are not our limp, neither are we our offences.

Sufis ask the question, "Is true repentance always being aware of one's sin or never being aware of one's sin?" Repentance, which means change, is usually thought of as feeling sorry for our misdeeds, accepting responsibility, *mea culpa*, and pledging never to do a repeat performance. But real change might mean that, along with being remorseful and resolving to make amends, we let go of our ego-based blame and trust that we are forgivable.

There is a sacred Self beneath the self that did or said what we regret – name it and claim it. If we fail to do so, if we choose to hold on to rather than let go of the self that is offended, we opt for an existence characterized by guilt and self-loathing that benefits no one. Words attributed to poet and author Maya Angelou are fitting here: "I did then what I knew how to do. Now that I know better, I do better."

# IN SYNC AND OUT OF STEP

When we let go of the self that is offended, we are at one with the sacred. Instead of reacting from our ego when we are offended, wounded, or hurt, we respond from our soul. Instead of getting even, we choose to go deeper into the mystery of our sacred Self, whence comes true forgiveness. Each time we are offended, whether by another or by ourselves, we are invited to let go of the self that remembers, to embrace true repentance, and to recommit to the spiritual journey, the dying process that is the relocation of our centre of gravity. Then we are no longer a "troubled guest on the dark earth," for we have died the death to our ego that is necessary to claim our place among those who live in the light.

# ELEVEN

# We Are Made to Have It All

*For Thou hast made us for Thyself and*
*our hearts are restless till they rest in Thee.*
— ST. AUGUSTINE

STATEMENTS LIKE "I WANT TO HAVE MY CAKE AND EAT IT TOO," "I want the best of both worlds," "It's my way or the highway," are usually thought to indicate that those who utter them are selfish. I was taught that people who want what they want when they want it cannot possibly care for others more than for themselves. The same applies to those who feel sorry for themselves when their needs are not met, or their preferences are not honoured. When a person is always "looking out for #1," the rest of us run a distant second.

To be honest, I am a person who wants what he wants, and I'm capable of sulking when I don't get my way. I've probably done a good job of hiding this fact and of trying to overcome it, but I am still prone to being the centre of my own universe and, when I can arrange it, other people's universes as well. I know I'm capable of feeling sorry for myself when my needs are not met, and I know I don't like who I am when I feel that way.

Doug, one of the people I serve as a spiritual director, came to a session feeling sorry for himself. He was conscious of the fact that there was a void in his life consisting of the absence of a significant other, and of his inability to befriend himself. Along with feeling empty inside, Doug was also judgmental about how he felt; he stated that his was a First World problem, and that he should be more grateful for the good things in his life. Like many of us, Doug's problems were compounded by his feeling bad about feeling bad, by feeling that he shouldn't be discontent.

## SELF-JUDGMENT IS NOT HELPFUL

Because I've known many "Dougs" through the years, and because I sometimes see him when I look in the mirror, I have given much thought to the inclination to judge ourselves for feeling upset when life is difficult, and for feeling bad about feeling bad. The conclusion I've come to is that whether caused by minor annoyances or major setbacks, the frustration, anger, impatience, and unhappiness we sometimes feel are not necessarily an indication that we are selfish or immature, though we are certainly capable of being so. Rather, they may be a reaction to the fact that the fullness we are created to experience eludes us.

I believe it is a holy and healthy instinct to be upset when we don't have what we desire, when we don't get our way, or when, for whatever reasons, we feel out of sorts. There is nothing wrong with feeling sad when we are lonely, mad when we are hurt, and disappointed when life doesn't cooperate with our plans. Because these feelings are not necessarily a sign that we are childish or selfish, they ought not to be judged and we ought not judge ourselves for having them. Instead, we should observe them and allow them to teach us about our spiritual birthright.

I realize the above statements may be confounding, for they seem to imply that it is virtuous to grasp for whatever we think will make us feel good, or to throw a tantrum when we are upset. But I am not, I repeat *not* advocating hedonism, condoning self-indulgence, or applauding immaturity. Rather, what I am emphasizing is the importance of looking more deeply into our yearning for the likes of pleasure, fulfillment, happiness, and satisfaction, because I believe they are an indication that we are spiritual by nature – these yearnings are a revelation of the truth that the "all" for which we are made is the infinite All most often referred to as God.

## HOLY DISCONTENT

Jesuit priest and mystic Teilhard de Chardin has said that we are not human beings having a spiritual experience, we are spiritual beings having a human experience. If we were the former, I think we would be happy with a life that granted only periodic satisfaction; we would be content with having a mere glimpse of glory – those fleeting moments when, for example, we sense the hidden wonder of life in the beauty of nature, the innocence of a child, or the kindness shown us by a stranger – and we would be less reactive in the face of life's many disappointments. But because we are first and foremost spiritual beings who are made to experience unending bliss, the times when we do not have this experience can lead us down the dark corridors of discontent.

Having said this, it is important to note the obvious; namely, that in a less-than-ideal world it is impossible to have our cake and eat it too. Neither is it possible, for the most part, to experience the bliss for which we are made without making other people's lives less blissful. And so, despite the fact that we are not selfish because we want what we want when we want it, it is selfish and offensive to demand or to take what we want in order to satisfy our needs.

Strange as it might sound, the corporate executive who cooks his company's books to pad his own pocket is, at some level, responding to an innate desire for ultimate satisfaction. However, he is doing this selfishly and at the expense of others, not to mention the fact that money can never bring about the joy for which our souls are made. The young man who is addicted to drugs is seeking a "high" for which he is created, but he is looking for it in an artificial way, one that cannot be sustained and that is harmful not helpful to himself and to society. The woman who seeks to alleviate her loneliness by moving from one unsatisfying relationship to another is likewise searching for the contentment that is her birthright, but again, the best of relationships cannot assuage the need for unconditional love we carry in our spiritual genes. Because our discontents have a spiritual origin, they can never be fulfilled by material possessions, physical pleasures, or emotional or relational satisfaction.

Someone who knows the insufficiency of the "good life," of having all we want, is author and artist Julia Cameron.

*I'm talking about my life: my cushy, privileged, nicer-than-most life. I have almost exactly the life I always said I wanted, and I don't really like it very much ... The point is that my life is stuffed to the gills with people, places, and things that ought to make me happy but they don't.*[1]

We are made to have it all. We are programmed for gratification. We may never be truly content with anything less than everything we desire, but what we often desire, what philosopher William James has called "the world's palliatives" – health, wealth, and happily-ever-after relationships – cannot do the job. George Bernard Shaw spoke to this truth when he opined that there are two great disappointments in life: one is to not get your heart's desire, and the other is to get it! While it is true that palliatives cannot satisfy our deepest longings, it is also important to recognize that the desire for fulfillment of our needs and for the elimination of what makes us discontent may be symptoms of a spiritual dis-ease.

Our spiritual birthright notwithstanding, it is important to realize that attempting to have the best of both worlds usually results in our being empty-handed. This truth is the moral of one of the fables told by the Greek storyteller Aesop. Aesop tells of a dog with a bone in its mouth that sees its reflection in a pond. Thinking it is another dog with a bigger bone, the animal lets go of its bone and tries to get the one it sees in the pond. Like that dog, we can end up with less than we have when we grasp for what seems bigger and better. Although being content with who we are and what we have is imperative, it is also good to keep in mind that there may be something spiritually fitting about experiencing a "holy discontent."

## UNSETTLED IS GOOD

Philosopher Ralph Waldo Emerson wrote that "People wish to be settled; only as far as they are unsettled is there any hope for them."[2] Settling down or settling into a relationship, a job, or a house, provides a sense of comfort and contentment, security and well-being. When these are missing from our lives, we may become anxious and apprehensive; states of mind and heart that adversely affect our ability to be fully functioning.

Given the importance of being settled, why would Emerson claim that being unsettled is something positive? I believe that when we feel unsettled, we tap into the basic truth that we are made to have it all. There is in each of us a longing that persists even when we have all that society claims we need to be happy. Like Doug and like Julia Cameron, most of us have a great deal to be grateful for, but if we remain still enough for long enough, there often lurks within us a sense of unsettledness.

My discontent and yours, if you are in touch with it, is at least to some degree existential in nature; it comes with the territory of being human; it arises from deep within. It is tempting to flee from this gnawing dis-ease, to get busy, to self-medicate, to find a quick fix that will offer a cure, or at least numb the inner ache. But rather than attempting to escape our discontent, it is better to allow ourselves to settle into the unsettledness, to hang around long enough for it to tutor our hearts; that is, to teach us who we are and why we are susceptible to it. Saint Augustine knew this proclivity had to do with our longing for God when he wrote, "For Thou hast made us for Thyself and our hearts are restless till they rest in Thee."[3]

As I have pondered my own unsettledness, I have come to realize that it is due not only to an unquenchable thirst for God, but also to the inescapable reality of impermanence. No matter how good I have it, what I have and who I am will one day cease to be. For many years I allowed the fear of losing what I love to keep me from embracing life and love.

Although I am less influenced by that fear now, I am still aware of the passing nature of life, and that I long for a permanent bliss I can never have on this earth. That longing tells me that I am made for more, and that I will never feel settled or content for long, not even with the best that life has to offer.

## THE GRASS IS BROWN ON BOTH SIDES

Imagination, and her twin sister fantasy, are powerful mental capacities that can transport us into a world that is worlds away from the one we occupy. Although they are siblings, imagination and fantasy differ significantly; the former is usually considered a positive force that enables one to see possibilities, to envision what has yet to be, while the latter is more often experienced as an escape from what has become difficult. Its negative connotation notwithstanding, it is because we are spiritual beings that we tend to fantasize.

The proverbial grass may not actually be greener beyond the fence that sometimes defines and at other times confines us, but it often looks that way from where we stand. When our life is less fulfilling or more painful than we would like, we may find ourselves fantasizing about a better life, creating in our minds what we think will give us the happiness we long for and for which we are made. If I had married that person instead of this one, I would be happier. If I had taken a different career path than the one I'm on, I would feel more fulfilled. If I owned a different house in a more affluent neighbourhood, life would be wonderful. In truth, our life *would* be different than it is had we made other choices, but we would probably still be discontent. The point is that our discontents are not necessarily a sign that we are malcontents; rather, they may be an indication that we are entitled by our spiritual nature to a contentment that will always be elusive.

We can choose to live in the lofty world of our fantasies, but sooner or later we will crash land. I was speaking with a friend who told me about a woman whom he found attractive. Although his fascination was based on appearance, his fantasies were more a matter of the mind and heart. Without ever having spoken with her, he presumed that she was emotionally mature, and that her opinions about religion, politics, and other social issues were as open-minded as his. In their first conversation, however, he found her to be very different from the person his fantasies had created, and much less attractive.

I believe that we make gods and goddesses of other people because we are made to be in the company of angels; heaven is our home even as we walk the earth. And although our fantasies reveal something about our spiritual nature and are, therefore, to be valued, it is best not to dwell on them but, instead, to embrace the sober reality of our lives and the holiness of our discontent.

It has been said that what each one of us reaches for may be different, but what makes us reach is the same. What we think will make us happy varies from person to person depending in large part on the messages we have received and the values we have learned from family, peers, faith communities, and society in general. But the inner longing for fulfillment that fuels our reaching, the hunger for wholeness, the craving for gratification, the homesickness for what is ultimate is universal, for each one of us is essentially spiritual; each one of us is made to have it all.

## IN SYNC AND OUT OF STEP

It is surely the sacred to which we respond when, instead of judging ourselves or others as selfish because we want a blissful life, we pause long enough to recognize the source of our longing; we are made to have it all. Society tells us to strive for what we desire and that, if we achieve what it values then we should feel settled. But the wisdom of a deeper self invites us to realize that because we are spiritual beings, we will always experience a "holy discontent," a yearning for what is out of reach, a hunger for what is ultimate and infinite. And although a life other than the one we're living may be appealing, that same wisdom suggests that we look deeper within to find the "greener grass" for which we long, the infinite All for which we are made.

# POSTSCRIPT

*If a man does not keep pace with his companions,*
*perhaps it is because he hears a different drummer.*
*Let him step to the music which he hears,*
*however measured or far away.*

— HENRY DAVID THOREAU

**I**F WE LISTEN WITH THE EAR OF OUR HEART, WE ARE LIKELY TO HEAR THE "DIFFERENT DRUMMER" TO WHICH THOREAU REFERS; it is the sound of the sacred that pulses through each of us, though we are not often attuned to it. This voiceless voice that some have called the "genius," "daemon," "sound of the genuine," and "True Self," summons us to authenticity; that is, to be true to the sometimes subtle but persistent urge to live while we are alive.

Life has been defined as a flicker of consciousness between two great silences. The origin of our being and our destiny beyond this life are impossible to comprehend, but what we know in our heart of hearts is that existence here on planet earth is too precious and too brief to live in a mindless, conventional manner that keeps us unaware of larger and deeper possibilities. We are travellers, sojourners, a people on the move, and when we step to the music of a different drummer, when we live in sync with the sacred, I believe we make the best use of the mystery of life with which we have been blessed.

The Hebrew scriptures invite us to "Be still, and know that I am God" (Psalm 46:10). Whatever our notion of the sacred may be, our best chance to connect with it usually comes when we are still and silent; two ways of being that, in the Western world, are countercultural. It is nothing short of radical to opt for stillness and silence in the midst of our "crazy busy" lives. But stillness need not mean stopping, and silence does not necessarily require the absence of sound.

Former United Nations Secretary General Dag Hammarskjöld claims that there is within each of us a still point surrounded by silence. The "spiritual journey" is the movement from surface to centre, from ego consciousness to the soulful awareness that there is something spiritual about us. When we are in touch with our soul, we can be still at the same time that we are going about the business required to survive and to thrive on a daily basis, and we can tap into the silent centre of ourselves in the midst of the world's ever-present racket.

It is a daily decision and discipline to live in sync with the sacred and out of step with the world, but if we make this manner of living a priority, both we and our corner of the world will be better for it.

# ACKNOWLEDGEMENTS

This book has been the work of minds and hearts other than my own. I dedicated it to my friend Ray DeFabio, without whose grammatical assistance and insightful feedback I could not have brought it to a satisfactory conclusion. There are more than a few references to Jim Finley, whom I identify as a friend, psychologist, former monk, and spiritual teacher. Jim's name appears on many of these pages, but his influence is on all of them. I am also indebted to Mike Schwartzentruber, my editor at Wood Lake Books. Mike offered many helpful suggestions that have served to make this a better book at the same time that he always honoured the fact that it was my book and my decision whether to accept his input. To these three, I say thank you.

# NOTES

### ONE | IF A THING IS WORTH DOING IT IS WORTH DOING BADLY

1. G. K. Chesterton, *The Collected Works of G. K. Chesterton,* vol. 4 (San Francisco: Ignatius Press, 1987), 199.
2. —. *Chesterton Collected Works*, vol. 13 (SanFrancisco: Ignatius Press, 2005), 409.

### TWO | LIFE IS NOT A ONE-PIECE PUZZLE

1. Coleman Barks, "The Guest House," *The Essential Rumi*, trans. Coleman Barks with John Moyne (SanFranciso: HarperOne, 2004), 109.
2. Robert Frost, "The Death of the Hired Man," *The Poetry of Robert Frost*, ed. Edward Connery Lathem (New York: Henry Holt and Company, Inc., 1979), 38.

### THREE | DON'T JUST DO SOMETHING, STAND THERE

1. Anthony de Mello, *The Song of the Bird* (New York: Image Doubleday, 1984), 15.
2. —. *Taking Flight* (New York: Image Doubleday, 1990), 35.

### FOUR | LIGHTEN UP

1. G. K. Chesterton, *Orthodoxy* (New York: Simon & Brown, 2016), 95.
2. George Bernard Shaw, *The Doctor's Dilemma* (Baltimore: Penguin Books, 1965), 185.
3. Roger Housden, *Ten Poems to Set You Free* (New York: Harmony Books, 2003), 27.

## FIVE | **PAIN IS INEVITABLE, SUFFERING IS AN OPTION**

1. Victor Frankl, *Man's Search for Meaning* (Boston: Beacon Press, 2006), 66.
2. James Baldwin, *I Am Not Your Negro* (New York: Vintage Books, 2017), 103.

## SIX | **OUR SOUL IS NONE OF OUR BUSINESS**

1. Stephen Mitchell, *The Enlightened Heart* (New York: HarperPerennial,1993), xv.
2. Robert Frost, "The Secret Sits," *The Poetry of Robert Frost*, ed. Edward Connery Lathem (New York: Henry Holt and Company, Inc., 1979), 362.
3. Roger Housden, *Ten Poems to Set You Free* (New York: Harmony Books, 2003), 125–26.
4. Coleman Barks, "A Great Wagon," *The Essential Rumi*, trans. Coleman Barks with John Moyne (San Francisco: HarperOne, 2004), 35.

## SEVEN | **WHATEVER IS HAPPENING SHOULD BE HAPPENING**

1. Robert Coles, *Dorothy Day: A Radical Devotion* (Reading, MA: Addison-Wesley Publishing Company, Inc., 1987), xviii.

## EIGHT | **THE VIRTUE OF HALF-HEARTED COMMITMENT**

1. Anaïs Nin, *The Diary of Anaïs Nin,* vol. 1 1931–1934, ed. Gunther Stuhlmann (New York: Houghton Mifflin Publishing Company, 1966), 137.

## NINE | **WE ARE MORE THAN OUR LIMP**

1. William Blake, *The Marriage of Heaven and Hell* (New York: Dover Publications, 1994), 36.
2. Annie Dillard, *Pilgrim at Tinker Creek* (New York: Harper Collins Publishers, Inc., 1974), 13.
3. Richard Bucke, *Cosmic Consciousness* ed. Richard Maurice Bucke. (Mansfield Centre, CT: Martino Publishing, 2010), 195.
4. Rainer Maria Rilke, *Letters to a Young Poet* (New York: Random House, 1984), 97.

## TEN | **LETTING GO OF AN OFFENCE MEANS LETTING GO OF THE SELF THAT IS OFFENDED**

1. Johann Wolfgang von Goethe, "The Holy Longing," *News of the Universe,* trans. Robert Bly (Berkeley: Counterpoint, 1980), 61.
2. Roger Housden, *Ten Poems to Set You Free* (New York: Harmony Books, 2003), 57.

## ELEVEN | **WE ARE MADE TO HAVE IT ALL**

1. Julia Cameron, *Prayers from a Nonbeliever* (New York: Jeremy Tarcher/Putnam, 2001), 7.
2. Ralph Waldo Emerson, *The Essential Writings of Ralph Waldo Emerson*, ed. Brooks Atkinson (New York: Modern Library, 2000), 261.
3. St. Augustine, *The Confessions of St. Augustine*, trans. F. J. Sheed (New York: Sheed & Ward, 1942), 3.

## POSTSCRIPT

1. Henry David Thoreau, *Walden* (New York: Alfred A Knopf, 1992), 288.

# BIBLIOGRAPHY

Augustine of Hippo. *The Confessions of St. Augustine.* New York, Sheed & Ward, 1942.

Baldwin, James. *I Am Not Your Negro.* New York: Vintage Books, 2017.

Barks, Coleman, ed. *The Essential Rumi.* San Francisco: HarperOne, 2004.

Becker, Ernest. *The Denial of Death.* New York: Macmillan Publishing Co. Inc., 1973.

Blake, William. *The Marriage of Heaven and Hell.* New York: Dover Publications, 1994.

Bly, Robert, trans. *News of the Universe.* Berkeley: Counterpoint, 1980.

Bucke, Richard, ed. *Cosmic Consciousness.* Mansfield Centre, CT: Martino Publishing, 2010.

Cameron, Julia. *Prayers from a Nonbeliever.* New York: Jeremy Tarcher/Putnam, Inc., 2001.

Chesterton, Gilbert Keith. *Orthodoxy.* New York: Simon & Brown, 2016.

—. *G. K. Chesterton Collected Works.* Vols. 4 and 13. SanFrancisco: Ignatius Press, 1987 and 2005.

Coles, Robert. *Dorothy Day: A Radical Devotion.* Reading, MA: Addison-Wesley Publishers, Inc., 1987.

de Mello, Anthony. *Taking Flight.* New York: Doubleday, 1990.

—. *The Song of the Bird.* New York: Image Doubleday, 1984.

Dillard, Annie. *Pilgrim at Tinker Creek.* New York: Harper Collins Publishers, Inc., 1974.

Emerson, Ralph Waldo. *The Essential Writings of Ralph Waldo Emerson.* New York: Modern Library, 2000.

Finley, James. *Christian Meditation*. San Francisco: HarperSanFrancisco, 2004.

—. "Merton's Path to the Palace of Nowhere." http://www.soundstrue.com/

Frankl, Victor. *Man's Search for Meaning*. Boston: Beacon Press, 2006.

Housden, Roger. *Ten Poems to Set You Free*. New York: Harmony Books, 2003.

Mitchell, Stephen. *The Enlightened Heart*. New York: HarperPerennial, 1993.

Nin, Anaïs. *The Diary of Anaïs Nin* Vol. 1 New York: Houghton Mifflin Publishing Company, 1966.

Rilke, Rainer Maria. *Letters to a Young Poet*. Translated by Stephen Mitchell. New York: Random House, 1984.

Shaw, George Bernard. *The Doctor's Dilemma*. Baltimore: Penguin Books, 1965.

Thoreau, Henry David. *Walden*. New York: Alfred A. Knopf, 1992.

# THE AUTHOR

Tom Stella has been sharing his spiritual wisdom with the world for years. A former priest in the Congregation of Holy Cross, he is the co-founder and director of Soul Link, Inc., a non-profit for spiritual seekers. He also serves as a spiritual director, retreat facilitator, and as a workplace chaplain for a health care system in Denver, Colorado. While a priest, Stella ministered in parishes, hospitals, hospices, and college campuses. His previous books include *The God Instinct* (Sorin Books), *A Faith Worth Believing* (HarperSanFrancisco), *Finding God Beyond Religion* (SkylightPaths), and *CPR for the Soul* (Wood Lake Publishing). He holds an MDiv degree from the University of Notre Dame, an MA in counselling from the University of Michigan, and an STM in spirituality from the Jesuit School of Theology in Berkeley.

## AWARDS AND RECOGNITION

· *The God Instinct* (Sorin Books, 2001) – a Spiritual Book Associates selection and winner of a Catholic Press Association First Time Author award
· *Finding God Beyond Religion* (SkylightPaths, 2013) – chosen as one of the 50 best books of 2013 by *Spirituality & Health* magazine
· *CPR for the Soul* (Wood Lake, 2017) – "Highly Recommended" in the Best Spiritual Author category, *Soul & Spirit's* Spiritual Book Awards, 2019

# CPR for the Soul

## REVIVING A SENSE OF THE SACRED IN EVERYDAY LIFE

### TOM STELLA

"The fact that you are not dead is not sufficient proof that you are alive!" So begins Tom Stella's insightful, important, and inspiring exploration into the life, death, and rebirth of the soul. He shares the deep, eternal wisdom that knows that the lines separating the sacred and the secular, time and eternity, humanity and divinity, are false. Or, at the very least, blurred. God, by whatever name, is found in the midst of everyday life, work, and relationships. All people, all creation, and all of life is holy ground. This remarkable book offers a revival for the soul, a reminder that "we are one with something vast" – a "something" that "is not a thing or a person, but a spiritual source and force at the heart of life."

ISBN 978-1-77343-039-3

5" X 8.5" | 248 PP | PAPERBACK | $19.95

# Passion & Peace

## THE POETRY OF UPLIFT
## FOR ALL OCCASIONS

### COMPILED BY DIANE TUCKER

All cultures we know of, at all times, have had poetry of one sort or another – chants, songs, lullabies, epics, blessings, farewells – to mark life's most important moments, transitions, and transformations. Ever since our species began using words, we have arranged them to please, to experience the pleasures, the fun, of rhythm and rhyme, repetition and pattern. *Passion & Peace: The Poetry of Uplift for All Occasions* was compiled to speak directly to this deep human need, with 120 poems from almost as many classical and contemporary poets, and including a thematic index. A welcome addition to any library and the perfect gift for any occasion, *Passion & Peace* is a heartwarming, uplifting, and inspirational volume.

ISBN 978-1-77343-028-7
6" X 9" | 304 PP | PAPERBACK | $24.95

# WOOD LAKE

## IMAGINING, LIVING, AND TELLING THE FAITH STORY.

### WOOD LAKE IS THE FAITH STORY COMPANY.

It has told
- the story of the seasons of the earth, the people of God, and the place and purpose of faith in the world;
- the story of the faith journey, from birth to death;
- the story of Jesus and the churches that carry his message.

Wood Lake has been telling stories for more than 35 years. During that time, it has given form and substance to the words, songs, pictures, and ideas of hundreds of storytellers.

Those stories have taken a multitude of forms – parables, poems, drawings, prayers, epiphanies, songs, books, paintings, hymns, curricula – all driven by a common mission of serving those on the faith journey.

### WOOD LAKE PUBLISHING INC.
485 Beaver Lake Road
Kelowna, BC, Canada v4v 1s5
250.766.2778

## www.woodlake.com